ITALIAN BLOWN GLASS

Venetian glass table-ware, in a fourteenth-century mosaic, detail from 'Herod's Feast' (1342-54)

Venice, Basilica di San Marco (Baptistery)

ITALIAN BLOWN GLASS

FROM ANCIENT ROME TO VENICE

BY GIOVANNI MARIACHER

McGRAW-HILL BOOK COMPANY INC.

NEW YORK · TORONTO · LONDON

Original title

Il Vetro Soffiato da Roma Antica a Venezia

Electa Editrice, Milan, Italy, 1960

Translation by Michael Bullock and Johanna Capra

© 1961 by Electa Editrice S.p.A.

Library of Congress Catalog Card Number: 61-15890

Printed in Italy

40360

TO THE MEMORY OF MY MOTHER

i BALM FLASK OF POURED VITREOUS PASTE WITH DECORATIONS IMITATING FEATHERS; RIBBED CUP OF COLOURED GLASS. ALEXANDRIAN ART (1ST CENTURY A. D.). ADRIA, MUSEO CIVICO. BULBOUS VESSEL AND DOUBLE HANGING BALM FLASK OF BLOWN GLASS. SYRIAN ART (1ST-2ND CENTURY A. D.). FORMERLY FORTUNY COLLECTION, NOW AT MURANO, MUSEO VETRARIO.

It might be said that a complete and satisfactory history of glass-making in Italy still remains to be written — a history which would clarify all obscurities, cover all the major and minor centres in which the art of glass-blowing was carried on, define all the varying local trends and specialities, and outline the commercial ties that existed with other countries. It is quite true that the origins and development of the art of glass-blowing were chiefly centred round Murano, a name which, at a certain point, became famous not only throughout the various regions of the Peninsula, but all over Europe, attracting the attention of experts everywhere. But it is also certain that glass workshops existed and flourished in other places besides the Venetian Lagoon. It will be enough to mention the name of Altare, a small village in Liguria, almost unknown yet the source of works of art and artists who spread Italian taste everywhere, especially in France and Flanders. Some very active workshops also flourished in many parts of Tuscany, including Florence itself. As for southern Italy, we know that the Neapolitan establishments were very successful, especially during the 16th and 17th centuries. In northern Italy, apart from Liguria, signs of activity are found in Lombardy, in Veneto (in Verona and Padua) and possibly elsewhere.

Unfortunately, there is not enough precise documentary and, above all, material evidence to testify in detail to the activity of the various centres, and so enable us accurately to reconstruct the whole history of glass-blowing. This demands a close search among the archives, together with a study of the centres of production and of the various written documents, whereby the origin of the various pieces now extant can be established with greater accuracy. All the same — as can be deduced from the bibliographical note below — some light has quite recently been cast on certain areas.

If, then, we wish to consider styles and techniques — which are naturally of great importance — we find ourselves on very difficult and uncertain ground. The main problem arises from the technique of glass-making itself, which, as far as Italian production is concerned, is identical everywhere, making differentiation impossible. The almost complete absence of specimens whose place of origin is firmly established — with the exception, of course, of those from Venice — is an added source of difficulty. A similar observa-

7

tion could be made about the late-Roman production; in fact, although its centres were various and situated in different parts of the Empire, the affinity of taste and technique makes reliable classification exceedingly difficult, if not impossible. Frequent commercial exchanges and the diffusion of the pieces exported, sometimes great distances from the places of origin, create further confusion. It is therefore clear that to write an accurate and well documented history of the manufacture of glass in Italy through the centuries is not an easy task in the present state of our knowledge. Until investigations still to be carried out have yielded further information, we must limit ourselves to a general survey, while trying to be as precise and informative as possible.

The art of glass-making, which from some points of view can be considered an industry of utilitarian character, is in other respects a true art, in the sense of a spontaneous creation that has issued from the human mind and is a product of technical skill, in the same way as a painting, a sculpture, a building or any other work of art. Moreover, it seems to us that the art of glass-making displays from its very first stages striking differences from other forms of industry or handicraft not only in its mode of expression. Although Pliny, the natural historian of antiquity, tried to reconstruct it for us, his story of the accidental invention of glass by Phoenician merchants is no doubt a poetic fiction; nevertheless, some truth must lie behind the legend, in the sense that the sand of the ancient river Belo, in Phoenicia, was very FIG. *i* suitable and sought after for the manufacture of glass, so that Syria played an important part in the development of the glass-making industry. Certainly Phoenician merchants and sailors were the chief instruments of distribution along the shores of the Mediterranean.

We also know that many of the most ancient specimens of glass that have been found originated from Egypt. It is still possible to study these finds; they are quite unmis-

takable, not merely because of their characteristic shapes and colours, but also because of the technique used in their manufacture. This technique consisted in shaping the glass when hot with the aid of a friable mould that was subsequently destroyed. The object was formed by pressing the molten vitreous paste round the mould. The usual method of decoration employed by the Egyptians was to wind different coloured threads of glass round the object while it was rotating. In this way they obtained the characteristic decorations of parallel and sometimes wavy stripes that may be seen on the cylindrical perfume caskets (*alabastra*) or on the small amphorae and vases PLS. of the *oinochoe* type found in tombs.

So far we have spoken only of articles manufactured of glass paste either pressed or poured into a mould. This method was extensively practised down to the 4th century, although it dates back to Dynasty XVIII (16th to 14th centuries B.C.); its diffusion was encouraged by trade between the Egyptians and Mediterranean nations such as the Greeks and Etruscans.

The art of glass-making as we know it today came into its own with the introduction of a new implement which revolutionised the manufacturing technique: the blowpipe. With blowing it became possible to create objects of a lightness and transparency such as had never been seen before. This discovery is generally thought to date from the beginning of the Christian era and its place of origin is believed to have been Syria. The composition of the vitreous material is based on a mineral substance (silica) alloyed with an alkali (soda) which serves as a founding medium. At a high temperature an amorphous material is obtained which assumes a brilliant red colour; in this soft pasty state it can be blown, stamped, used to weld two other pieces together, drawn into fine threads, or poured into moulds, cut with scissors, and modelled *ad libitum*, until it cools down. The cooling must, however, proceed by stages, so as to avoid upsetting the stability of molecular co-

8

hesion, which might easily result in breakage. For this reason the objects are removed to successive cooling chambers until they are adjusted to the surrounding temperature. The glass may be colourless or appropriately tinted in its actual substance by the addition of particular chemicals, generally metallic oxides, with which it is possible to obtain the most varied hues, ranging from bright red to blue, green, milky white, opaline and so on (a technique already known to glass-makers of the 1st century). Transparency, on the other hand, is obtained by purifying the material of scoria by means of appropriate substances. The Muranese glass-makers used manganese dioxide, the Bohemians and the British employed strong admixtures of lead and potassium oxides for their crystal. The object can be ornamented when the glass is cold, either without first reheating it, or else in such a way that the colour is vitrified in its turn. The latter method produces a true enamel painting, characteristic of certain Oriental (Syrian) and Venetian decorative techniques, as we shall see later.

Glass is therefore an amorphous material, but unlike pottery, cannot be moulded until it is incandescent. Melting takes place in special furnaces, generally circular in shape and provided with several external openings or 'working holes'; behind each working hole the compounds are melted in large pots at a very high temperature (2000-2500 C.). From these pots the master glass-blower takes on the end of his pipe a small amount of glass, called the *bolo*, in a fluid and slightly viscous state. Then he blows into the pipe and adds the finishing touches with the aid of a very few simple tools. This method has remained virtually unchanged since the invention of the blowpipe, which still represents the chief implement in the art of glass-making. Likewise, the other tools, perfect in their simplicity, have remained much the same throughout the centuries. They are in essentials identical with those enumerated by A. Neri in his magnificent *Trattato dell'Arte Vetraria* (1612), namely a

few types of pincers, scissors, and some flat wooden spatulas which are used to shape and mould the articles. The glass-maker sits on a special stool or on a wooden bench having next to him a shelf on which to rest the blowpipe during the various delicate processes of manufacture. As we have said, the molten glass can be moulded into any shape and parts can be added or taken away as required. It is during this initial phase that rims or handles can be attached to vases and the bases or the stems of chalices are adjusted. Decorations previously prepared can also be applied at this stage, as they easily adhere to the surface still softened by heat. Glass-blowing is difficult in spite of its basic simplicity because it depends entirely upon the free-hand manipulations of the glass-maker; it is sometimes a long and complex process and requires great skill and patience.

In addition to the efficiency of the tools and the technique, which has not changed for centuries, questions of an aesthetic order naturally enter into the process of manufacture. Hence, it is no surprise to find a curious and sometimes unexpected continuity between modern and ancient glass, as for instance between shapes and styles peculiar to Roman craftsmanship and those which are characteristic of Murano during the Middle Ages or the Renaissance. This becomes fully manifest when we re-examine some of the most typical aspects of glass-making in antiquity. Let us begin with the commonest vessel of everyday, utilitarian, purpose: the bottle.

We see a great variety of types: some square in section with a flattened base and a stumpy neck; some having a simple broad handle, like a band, added to the upper part. Some bottles had a slender and graceful shape with the body tapering toward the base and a long neck with slightly lipped rim. In some specimens the neck was much longer than the bottle itself; the result was strange but not without a certain elegance. This type of bottle, usually of small proportions, was chiefly used as a container for oils and resinous substances.

PLS. 7, 9-12, 14

FIG. X

PL. 12

ii PORTLAND VASE, IN CAMEO TECHNIQUE. ALEXANDRIAN ART (1ST CENTURY A. D.). LONDON, BRITISH MUSEUM.

With the aid of special wooden or earthenware moulds, it was possible to obtain geometrical shapes. The underside of the base was often FIG. *viii* printed with a seal consisting of initials or a portrait, real trade-marks which sometimes also bore the name of the craftsman and even of the locality, generally Sidon, the Syrian city already known to Pliny and one of the most active centres of the glass-making industry in antiquity. It is a curious fact that PL. 14 such glasses have actually been excavated in places very distant from one another. For example, glasses stamped 'Ennius' have been found in various localities and so have small bottles bearing an image of Mercury, of which the specimens now at Cologne and in the FIG. X Museo Civico in Bologna are reproduced in the present volume.

Pliny describes in great detail the various techniques employed by the Romans. Among the extraordinary variety of types and styles to be found in all the different provinces of the Empire, we can often observe shapes borrowed from the contemporary art of metal-casting. To quote one example: the *pterotos* type of cup in vogue during the 1st century, characterised by two wing-like handles and having the typical flattened prominence at the top and a small round base, is found reproduced in glass vessels of very similar shape during the 1st and 2nd centuries A.D. Moreover, the technique used for casting metals seems to have inspired the procedure of pouring molten glass into a mould and subsequently polishing it with a grindstone. Although rare, objects of this type are exhibited in a few museums. Plate I shows a two-handled amphora decorated with concentric intagliated rings. It is of thick greenish glass, but the surface looks smooth and silky thanks to the extremely fine polishing with emery. This object, now the pride of the Bologna museum, is considered to be of Phoenician manufacture, but to have been imported by the Etruscans. It was found in one of the Felsinian tombs dating from the end of the 6th century. It is still doubtful whether the Etruscans produced glass or whether the objects found in their tombs, such as the balm flasks of vitreous paste so similar to the Egyptian ones, had not been imported as a result of their trading activities, especially with the Eastern world. However, as we shall see, the fact remains that the grindstone, widely employed for those glasses which seem to have been intended to compete with the most precious metals, came increasingly to be used for cut glass, especially that produced in Alexandria. Alexandrian glasses, of which there were a great variety and wealth of types, achieved an unparalleled refinement and perfection, and since the wealthy Romans competed for their possession they came to fetch very high prices. This is particularly true of the so-called 'murrhine' glass. We do not know exactly what this was, in spite of the enthusiastic but vague allusions to it made by historians, but the name appears to have designated multicoloured

FIG

PL.

PL.

PL.

PL.

FIG

glassware obtained by mixing together minute pieces of very bright colours (like a molten mosaic), or else imposing variegated glass canes on a glass plate. The design was in the form of a cross or a star, or, in any case, of some shape radiating from a centre, and after melting the articles — cups, small pots or boxes shaped like pyxes — presented a wonderful decorative effect. Such vessels, together with other multicoloured glasses later referred to as *millefiori*, or glass of a thousand flowers, are to be seen in various Italian and foreign museums devoted to the exhibition of archaeological finds.

Between the 2nd and 6th centuries the centre of manufacture of such objects shifted to the estuary of the River Nile. The products of this new centre were in great demand, perhaps because of the predilection for colour in the ancient world or because they were reminiscent of the pressed glass that had been manufactured, as we have seen, in the Egypt of the Pharaohs and even after the Roman conquest. Although this was a rarer phenomenon — or so it would seem from the specimens now extant — we already find in this centre of manufacture the employment of a technique which Eastern craftsmen, and later the Venetians themselves, were to revive — the technique of enamel decoration.

This short and necessarily condensed outline of ancient glass-making will not appear a superfluous digression when we bear in mind the frequently surprising traces of these older traditions still visible in later periods. None of the techniques employed in artistic glass-making was unknown to the Ancients. Apart from true 'blown' glass and the production of utilitarian ware — in which, however, aesthetic considerations were never ignored — the Roman Empire was characterised by a continual search for new processes of increasing complexity and extravagance, for instance intaglio. Starting from the early methods of engraving glass by cutting into its surface with a stone wheel, we come, centuries later, to those marvellous

iii HORN-SHAPED DRINKING VESSEL OF PALE AMBER TRANSLUCENT GLASS. ROMAN ART (C. 1ST CENTURY A. D.). ADRIA, MUSEO CIVICO.

glasses called *diatreta* — generally goblets or ceremonial drinking vessels — which appear to have been made out of two layers of glass, of which the inner one was entirely smooth and the outer one perforated but leaving many points of contact with the inner layer. The famous goblet that once belonged to the Trivulzio Collection and is now in the Castello Sforzesco, Milan, a similar goblet exhibited in the Strasbourg Museum, and a pail or *situla* belonging to the Treasury of St. Mark's, Venice, are three of the very few examples still extant that give us some idea of this technique.

The extreme patience and skill of the craftsman aided only by the grindstone enabled him to cut through the thickness of the glass until it became, so to speak, two objects, one within the other, the outer serving as a protection to the inner, with hatched open-work patterns and sometimes with small figures — as can be seen in the example at St. Mark's — or

11

bearing dedicatory inscriptions. The artists who devoted themselves to this particular craft were usually Alexandrians and many of them had moved their workshops to Rome itself. It seems that their art flourished especially between the 1st and 4th centuries A.D. until more expeditious systems came into fashion, such as the application of ornaments or figures moulded separately and subsequently welded to the surface of the glass. In this way the so-called *pseudo-diatreta* were created, of which specimens have been found in the Catacombs or cemeteries of the Early Christian period. In some cases patterns of a geometrical nature — lines, dashes, circles — were incised in the polished surface. In others the incised decorations were figures illustrating mythological scenes, such as Venus and Cupid (on the conical glass at the Bonn Museum) or Bacchus and Ariadne, *putti*, satyrs and the like.

The intaglio technique was also utilised by the glass-makers to imitate cameos. For this purpose they worked on glass made of two layers of two different colours, generally white and pale blue, thereby achieving striking effects of contrast. We need only think of the splendid examples housed in the British Museum (the so-called Portland Vase) and the Museo Nazionale, Naples — both the work of Alexandrian artists dating from around the 1st century. Another typical technique, quite widespread among the Romans and reserved especially for objects of everyday use, was that of pressing. The same procedure was employed for marking the bottoms of bottles and for shaping the stems of chalices as was practised by Muranese glass-makers in the 16th century. It could also be used as a quick and simple method of shaping objects that had been blown: for the most part small bottles sometimes shaped like bunches of grapes or sometimes like human heads, small vases or balm flasks, certainly inspired by contemporary terracottas, in the shape of women's heads, bearded gods or grotesque caricatures. Finally, before leaving this group, we must recall the small flat shell-shaped bottles, and

the flasks for balms and perfumes shaped like birds, in which the body was drawn out to a point, producing an extremely graceful effect.

We have thus passed in review, even if briefly, the most characteristic elements of Roman production in its heyday. Early Christian art, following in the footsteps of pagan tradition, took over its types and forms and was its first great heir in the field of glass-making. Many shapes passed over either into liturgical use, such as chalices, goblets, vials and so on, or into the funerary cult, through which medium they have come down to us. It will be enough to recall the copious group of glasses with a golden base decorated with figures, portraits, scenes or dedicatory texts, and also the continuation of free-hand engraving on plates, baptismal mugs, and chalices, the only change being the iconography.

Golden bases may be considered one of the most curious and characteristic activities in the glass-making of the late Roman world. These articles are nothing but ordinary glasses and cups with a low base on which extremely thin gold leaf has been applied. On this gold leaf the craftsman incised the subject of his representation — sacred objects, portraits of important personages or mythological allegories. After the gold leaf had been applied and trimmed and some small areas of the gold removed so as to produce an open-work design, a second layer of glass was superimposed, creating a double bottom. This second layer of glass was often coloured — green, red or deep blue — so that it formed a strong contrast with the gold. This technique was widely employed and the result was often striking. Many specimens have come down to us excavated particularly from pagan or Early Christian tombs, although in the majority of cases they consist only of fragments or merely the base. Several Italian and foreign museums own interesting specimens; for instance the collections of the Biblioteca Vaticana in Rome and of the Museo Cristiano in Brescia. These pieces are generally believed to date from the 3rd

FIG. *ii*

FIG. *viii*

PLS. 7, 10, 13, 14

iv TWO AMPULLAE WITH HANDLES, OF SPOTTED GLASS AND OF POLYCHROME PASTE. ROMAN ART (1ST-2ND CENTURY A. D.). ADRIA, MUSEO CIVICO.
v BOWL OF 'MURRHINE' GLASS AND CASKET WITH LID OF 'MILLEFIORI' GLASS, POLISHED WITH THE GRINDSTONE. ALEXANDRIAN ART (1ST CENTURY A. D.). ADRIA, MUSEO CIVICO.

vi TWO CYLINDRICAL VASES OF BLACK AND WHITE VITREOUS PASTE MOULDED WHILE HOT (FROM A TOMB NEAR ADRIA). PRE-ROMAN ART (4TH–3RD CENTURY B. C.). ADRIA, MUSEO CIVICO. *vii* TWO-HANDLED CUP BLOWN INTO A MOULD AND FINISHED WITH THE GRINDSTONE, IMITATING THE 'PTEROTOI' VASES IN STYLE. ALEXANDRIAN ART (1ST–2ND CENTURY A. D.). ADRIA, MUSEO CIVICO.

and 4th centuries A.D. The Catacombs have also yielded many objects of a more usual kind of greenish transparent glass, such as the jugs called 'of the Martyrs' blood', and various types of drinking glasses, small hanging lamps, and reliquaries.

But we must return for a moment to our previous subject. It is by now clear that the extensive range of articles made in glass by the Romans, and distributed all over the ancient world, fall into two clearly distinct categories. The first includes all those common articles which have no specific identification marks and are therefore difficult to classify, so that even when the site of discovery is known, it still remains impossible to establish their place of origin because of the frequent and widespread commercial exchanges between the various regions of the Empire. The second category comprises all those items of high quality intended for ceremonial purposes and created as works of art. It naturally includes all glasses made of molten mosaic or canes (murrhine glass), coloured, enamelled, engraved, incised, intagliated glass (*diatreta*) and all glass vessels shaped by hand without the aid of moulds, which were, on the contrary, widely employed for the more utilitarian types of glassware. The particularly refined quality of these artistic glasses suggests an affinity with the high-grade products of Alexandrian, Greek or more generally Hellenistic manufacture dating from the 1st to the 4th century A.D.

It is therefore of great interest and significance for further developments to note that during Roman times, in the course of the early to the late Empire period, utilitarian glassware everywhere acquired certain common characteristics, almost an identity of types and techniques, precisely parallel to what happens in modern industrial mass production. This, rather than any other factor, explains the similarities of types to be observed among pieces of this period even when they originate from such different places as Southern Italy, Gaul, the Iberian peninsula, Germany or England.

After the decline of the Western Empire, when Rome lost its position as a centre of attraction, the manufacture of glass also underwent those vicissitudes and changes which characterised the emergence of new civilisations in Europe. Most interesting of all is the tendency for the various provinces to evolve an autonomy which was finally to produce articles of divergent types, which naturally differed in quality and importance, but were typical of the various different regions — the Iberian Province, England, France, Belgium, Holland, the Scandinavian countries and even distant Russia (especially the districts of the Caucasus and Ukraine). In Europe the major activity seems to have centred in the Rhineland, where glass-making already flourished in Roman times.

Techniques and shapes, even where they sprang from the convergence of different civilisations, seem in general to have been bound up with the inheritance of late Roman times to produce a trend in manufacture which tended to concentrate on utilitarian ware, abandoning almost completely the production of objects of high quality. Certain shapes enjoyed particular favour, for example the Merovingian and Carolingian conical glasses. Finally, we see the predominance of decorations which can be applied, such as the glass drops or embossed patterns typical of the glasses called by the Germans *Römer* (known in English as 'rummers'), which were widely diffused during the Gothic era. As a result, perhaps, of the shortage of certain raw materials, these vessels do not display the same refinement of quality as we see in ancient glass; the glass of which they are made is rather coarse and mostly brown or greenish in colour, as is the case with the *Waldglas*, or 'forest glass', produced in Germany, especially during the 14th century.

Meanwhile the provinces of the Byzantine Empire, which seem to have remained more faithful to the Roman inheritance than the West, continued to produce artistic objects based upon Hellenistic or Alexandrian models.

PLS. 18, 19

15

PHIOLE.

M.ʳ le Marq. de Caumont.

viii BOTTLE FOR EVERYDAY ˙ ˙ ˙ N INTO A MOULD, WITH INITIAL
LETTERS AND TRADE MARK ON BASE. SYRIAN ART. FROM AN 18TH CEN-
TURY WATERCOLOUR BY GREVENBROECK. VENICE, MUSEO CORRER.

ix ROMAN DRINKING VESSEL. FROM AN 18TH CENTURY WATERCOLOUR
BY GREVENBROECK. VENICE, MUSEO CORRER.

They still made murrhine glass, the moulded
glass ornamented with applied decorations and
imitations of precious stones anticipating the
famous Venetian *conterie* or fancy glass. The
outstanding centre for the manufacture of
enamelled glass, on the other hand, was Syria,
whose products remained typical throughout
the whole of the 14th century and were influenced more by the new expanding Islamic culture than by Byzantium. The latter continued
and extended the use of glass tesserae for the
art of mosaic, which was to enjoy considerable
favour in the Italian territories subject to the
Exarchate and to Venice.

It is now time to inquire into the position of
glass-making in Italy during the high Middle
Ages. We do not know for certain how long
antique manufacture continued or how long the
tradition was preserved, which was certainly
transmitted from Rome to centres that were already active at that time, such as Latium and
the Campanian workshops which utilised the
sands of the Volturno, and in the North those
of Aquileia and, perhaps, of Adria. But meanwhile, throughout the dramatic and confused
vicissitudes of the barbarian invasions and the
rise of various new civilisations, glass, like the
other industrial arts, seems to be seeking new
directions. Although glass production was rare
and sporadic, it still continued in an attempt
to satisfy the demands of everyday life. Finally, account must be taken of the fact that
the craftsmen, like the objects themselves,
moved about and tended to take part in a
migration from East to West, assisting the
broad expansion of the currents of Islamic and
Moorish art either in the Northern Adriatic
— especially in Venice — or in Southern Italy
and Sicily, as may be seen from the diffusion
of particular architectural and decorative forms
in the 12th and 14th centuries.

The art of mosaic seems to have aided and
fostered the development of a parallel industry: the manufacture of glass tesserae in the
most varied colours and combinations of colours. It is not, of course, certain that in

every place where the churches were decorated with mosaics there was also a workshop producing glass tesserae; on the other hand it is more than likely that this was so in the case of certain areas, such as Ravenna and district and the Venetian Lagoon itself. We know that in Ravenna, the capital of Byzantine Italy, the mosaic tradition continued right into the 12th century. There can be no doubt that this tradition found its way to the Venetian estuary, although there is no concrete evidence to this effect. It is however a fact that Torcello reveals traces of mosaic decorations in its Cathedral, part of which dates from the Ravenna period, that is to say from the 7th century. Inheriting the cultural and political patrimony of Ravenna, and linked for a time with Byzantium, Venice practised the art of mosaic on a considerable scale, employing it during the first few centuries as the chief, if not the only vehicle, for the expression of its figurative vision. Many of the Venetian churches, in addition to St. Mark's basilica itself, were already embellished with mosaics between the 9th and the 12th centuries. Principally for this reason, and taking into account the fact that the first glass-makers appear in the 11th century, it has been deduced that the first Venetian workshops were built for the manufacture of glass tesserae. This thesis, though not altogether implausible, is also not entirely convincing. We have here one of the major problems that confront us in the history of Italian glass in general and Venetian glass in particular. If we may, in fact, believe that workshops devoted to utilitarian articles continued their activity in other regions, and particularly in those centres of Roman origin (Rome itself, the Campanian centres and perhaps others in Northern Italy), the case of Venice was entirely different. Scholars are no longer under any illusion as to the possibility of direct Roman influences or indirect influences from the centres of population which sprang up following the barbarian invasion. The new centres were truly born from nothing, the Lagoon was undeveloped and almost uninhabited without signs of

x THREE GLASS VESSELS FOR EVERYDAY USE (CRUETS). ROMAN ART (1ST-2ND CENTURY A. D.). BOLOGNA, MUSEO CIVICO.

any previous civilisation which would enable us to trace a line of development leading back to a Roman origin. We, therefore, have no alternative but to consider the neighbouring areas of the mainland, where some degree of continuity may still be visible: Altino, Eraclea, Grado and also, although it is not so close, the rich and important trading centre of Aquileia, at that time a river-port, though almost a sea-port by virtue of its proximity to the Adriatic. It was certainly one of those centres of population which continued for some time to retain elements of an Imperial inheritance while the barbarian invasions were taking place. In a certain sense, Aquileia had a share in the origins of Venice as did the centres of Roman origin closer to the shores of the Lagoon. The same could be said of Grado, residence of the Patriarchate, and in its turn a place of refuge for those fleeing from Aquileia

17

and one town after another all the way down the Via Emilia Altinate, the highway which runs from Este and Padua, almost following the Adriatic coast and leading, even today, towards Trieste and the Via Postumia. The products of a prosperous industry such as that of glass-making must have spread along the consular highways that were open for communications and commercial traffic during the Roman era; the numerous pieces of documentary evidence and archaeological finds are the best possible testimony to this, and the Aquileian museum is certainly one of the richest in glassware. Hence the hypothesis of the existence in Aquileia itself (which is confirmed by literary references), and in the neighbourhood, of workshops for the manufacture of utilitarian glassware, is bound up with the industry of mosaic glass tesserae. It must not be forgotten that this pictorial technique was used not only on the nearby mainland — at Padua and Vicenza, for example — but also in various monuments on the Venetian and Istrian coasts from Torcello to Parenzo. But it must be added that before it could be regarded as firmly established such a hypothesis would require the support of some concrete evidence, whereas no archaeological find has yet come to light to provide definite evidence of the existence of glass furnaces, no fragments or debris of molten glass or other definite material remains have been unearthed. Nevertheless, the hypothesis that such furnaces existed cannot be completely dismissed when we take account of all the upheavals resulting from the rapid succession of events, with the advent of new civilisations, the flight of the Venetians to the Lagoons and the progressive abandonment, and finally the total destruction, of flourishing centres such as Altino, Concordia and Eraclea.

As the reader will have gathered, the problem is a thorny one and scholars certainly cannot be said to have reached an entirely satisfactory conclusion. However, another recent theory should be mentioned (Gasparetto, 1958, see Bibl.) which carries some conviction.

As is well known, even during the dark period that characterised the High Middle Ages in Italy, a bright torch of civilisation was kept burning amidst the turmoil of events. This tenuous but uninterrupted spark of civilisation was preserved by the monastic communities and religious Orders, especially the Benedictines, to whom is due the diffusion of architectural forms and also of certain distinct pictorial trends. The same could be said of miniatures, the transcription of the *Codices* and the creation of very well stocked libraries. In such activities we may observe the particular proclivity of the monks for undertakings of a technical and handicraft character, such as book-binding, weaving, goldsmith's work and also glass-making, possibly carried out with the aid of small furnaces. It will be enough to remember that the most important technical treatise of the time — *Schedula diversarum artium* — was written by a monk in a Cologne monastry towards the middle of the 10th century, and that this treatise remains today a celebrated source of precise and detailed information regarding the art of glass-making. However, even if we assume the existence of a preliminary period of experimental activity by the monks and makers of glass tesserae for mosaics — activities which were quite independent of each other — it has been proved that Venetian glass-makers were already active before A.D. 1000. These craftsmen were called *phioleri* because they blew phials.

Perhaps the answer to the old problem of the origin of glass-making in Italy is not to be found in any one of the many proposed solutions, but in the convergence of the various early experimental enterprises to form a true tradition. On the one hand there is the diffusion of common vessels such as flasks, drinking glasses, jugs and bottles, often blown with the aid of a mould — in which connection there is a curious portrayal, in an 18th century Venetian water-colour by Grevenbroeck, of a moulded glass *phiola* of Syrio-Roman type which is reminiscent of specimens found in

FIG

xi

xii

xiii

xi BOTTLES AND HOUR GLASS. DETAIL FROM 'ST JEROME IN HIS STUDY' BY COLANTONIO (MID-15TH CENTURY). NAPLES, MUSEO NAZIONALE.
xii ITALIAN TABLE GLASSES FROM A FRESCO OF THE CONTEMPORARY BOLOGNESE SCHOOL (14TH CENTURY). POMPOSA, ABBAZIA. *xiii* WATER BOTTLE. DETAIL FROM 'ST JEROME IN HIS STUDY' BY COLANTONIO (MID-15TH CENTURY). NAPLES, MUSEO NAZIONALE.

xiv

xv

xvi

xiv EXAMPLE OF 'A FREDDO' (UNHEATED) PAINTING ON GLASS: DETAIL FROM A SCENE WITH MARINE DEITIES IN THE DECORATION OF A BOWL (LATE 16TH CENTURY). MURANO, MUSEO VETRARIO .*xv* PILGRIM'S FLASK OF THE 'TERRASANTA' TYPE, AN EXAMPLE FROM THE END OF THE 16TH CENTURY (?). VENICE, SALVIATI-CAMERINO COLLECTION. *xvi* FLASK PAINTED WITH POLYCHROME ENAMELS. SPANISH ART (BARCELONA) FROM THE END OF THE 15TH CENTURY. MURANO, MUSEO VETRARIO.

xvii

xviii

xix

xvii TABLE GLASSES IN A 'LAST SUPPER' BY BONIFACIO VERONESE (16TH CENTURY). BASSANO, MUSEO CIVICO. *xviii* CRYSTAL GOBLET WITH BALUSTRADED STEM. VENETIAN ART (16TH CENTURY). MURANO, MUSEO VETRARIO. *xix* BOWL-SHAPED CRYSTAL GOBLET WITH EMBOSSED PATTERN. VENETIAN ART (16TH CENTURY). LONDON, VICTORIA AND ALBERT MUSEUM.

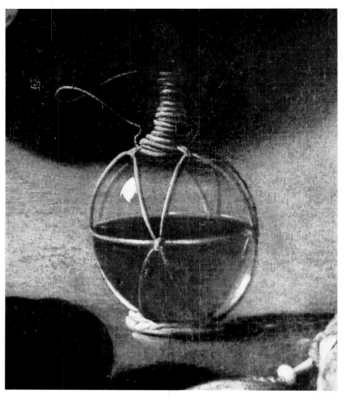

XX STRAW-ENCASED BOTTLE FOR POPULAR USE. DETAIL FROM 'THE COOK IN THE KITCHEN' BY THE SCHOOL OF CARAVAGGIO (17TH CENTURY). FLORENCE, GALLERIA CORSINI. *XXI* FLOWER VASE FROM A 'PORTRAIT OF A WOMAN' BY PARIS BORDONE (16TH CENTURY). TURIN, GALLERIA SABAUDA. *XXII* TABLE BOTTLE AND CUP WITH HANDLE, FROM THE 'SUPPER OF SAN CARLO BORROMEO' BY DANIELE CRESPI (17TH CENTURY). MILAN, CHURCH OF SANTA MARIA DELLA PASSIONE.

Venice or its environs and, hence, further evidence in favour of the theory that a late-Roman civilisation existed on the nearby mainland. On the other hand, we cannot exclude the possibility that the craft of glass-making — as happened with other crafts — was introduced to the Lagoon by communities of monks who had a few quite important monasteries in Venice itself and on many of the small islands from the earliest centuries of the Christian era onward. Finally, the increasing demand for glass tesserae for mosaic work — tesserae which were in earlier periods imported from the Eastern Byzantine provinces — led to the establishment of local workshops for reasons of convenience and economy. Once these workshops had been established, additional activities had to be found to keep them occupied, which gave a further impetus to the whole glass-making industry. Factors of a technical nature should not be overlooked either, because they afford evidence of the undoubted connection between the new Venetian manufacture and the ancient tradition.

We could start by considering a piece, the date of which, however, is not absolutely certain: a modest but interesting jug which reminds us, in its simple but functional shape, of similar objects in terracotta, with a flat bottom and a broad, ribbon-like handle; this jug was blown in a rather impure glass and is of somewhat crude manufacture. It was found in the last century at the bottom of a canal on the island of Murano itself, and after rejecting the hypothesis that it might even be Roman, scholars finally attributed it to the local industry, possibly of the 14th century. There is unfortunately insufficient evidence to date it more precisely. If the hypothesis of its local manufacture is accepted, we must infer that at that time only objects of everyday use and rather commonplace character were produced. This inference, on the other hand, accords with the historical data contained in all the documentary material that has come down to us. The numerous names of *phioleri* transmitted to us by archives, the existence of a statute — already revised in 1271 — the special laws passed by the government, references in chronicles and other documents, down to the famous order promulgated by the Maggior Consiglio (the Senate) in 1291 demanding the removal of all workshops from within the city boundaries to the nearby island of Murano, are all elements in an historical outline which will grow increasingly clear as time goes by. The concentration of all workshops on Murano is certainly the most important act in the history of Venetian glass-making and the starting point of what has since become the monopoly of the island. Further measures were taken which brought something approaching independence to this island that had already been prosperous during the 7th - 9th centuries, as is proved by its most important monument, the basilica of Sts. Maria and Donato, also decorated with mosaics. The Muranese had their own Government representative, the Gastaldo (or Bailiff) and later, since 1275, a mayor, whose authority was equal to that of the Doges. They had their own Council and nobility, who were naturally the aristocracy of glass-makers, inscribed in a Golden Book. The possibility of family ties with the Venetian nobility facilitated relations with the Rialto, while at the same time they maintained a splendid isolation. Finally, Murano struck commemorative medals, called *oselle*, to celebrate each election of a Doge in St. Mark's; these medals bore the coats of arms and initials of the representatives of the island.

These facts are exceptionally interesting from a political point of view as well. We may suppose that a flourishing and well organised industrial activity went hand in hand with the growing power and self-confident independence of the Muranese people, as is borne out by the various regulations; for instance the regulations controlling apprenticeships, the sale, import and export of glass, and above all the emigration of craftsmen. This becomes evident when we read the *Mariegola*, or body of laws affecting craftsmen, first issued in the 13th century but revised in 1441, the date of the edition that has come down to us. Murano soon contributed to the economic prosperity of its neighbour Venice. We know that its products went far beyond its boundaries and the whole Adriatic coast. Chronicles and histories have brought us lively accounts of great successes. The gorgeous ceremonies that took place on the occasion of the Doge's coronation were often accompanied by processions of the different corporations of craftsmen, a real parade of the Venetian industries. We learn from Martino da Casale's account of the ceremony in honour of Lorenzo Tiepolo (1268) that even at this early date the glass-makers took part, exhibiting a rich variety of objects. Due to the ravages of time, however, no object of absolutely certain provenance has come down to us. It is not until we reach the middle of the 15th century that we come upon objects of Venetian manufacture whose origin we can confidently accept. It is not surprising that from this date onward, discussion of Italian glass-making deals chiefly with the activity of the Lagoon workshops. The history of glass-blowing in Italy, as we have said, is in fact virtually synonymous with the history of glass-blowing on Murano, especially if we are considering production of high-quality articles on a large scale. Hence we shall concentrate primarily upon the Muranese craftsmen. Their work is generally anonymous, but the character of their artistic expression, which has been maintained for centuries, will enable us to trace the whole history of glass-making in Italy. Naturally, we shall concern ourselves mainly with works of art and the qualities appertaining to them.

We now come to the earliest specimens which have reached us intact and which afford the first concrete evidence of a maturity of style. They are not objects of everyday use; in fact it was impossible for many of the latter to be preserved intact on account of the fragility of their material. On the contrary, the extant objects consist of exceptional pieces, created to order for special purposes — engagement or wedding presents, liturgical vessels and so on. These surviving objects are chiefly goblets, cups or glasses, plates, bowls and similar articles. Because of the special purposes for which they were made these vessels were intended as works of art and for the most part stand out as considerably superior aesthetically to the general level of the craftwork of their time. They were particularly refined in shape, material and decoration. As for the shape, it seems that this was often borrowed from metal or earthenware objects of the same period — an analogous situation to that which occurred in Roman times. We find goblets with a high base like those in the Bologna museum, which have a conical base with an upturned rim, a spherical knot, the lower part of the body decorated with prominent ribs (obtained, of course, with the aid of a mould), while the upper part is circular and polished, reproducing the characteristics of metal goblets. The same phenomenon can be observed in all the cups of this kind, and also in those with a low base exhibited in the museums of Florence, Stuttgart, Paris, London, Cologne and elsewhere. In such objects every detail recalls the objects made of copper or precious metals during the Gothic period, with either embossed or hammered or intagliated patterns, prominent ribs, knots and crenellated edges. Finally, but far from being the least important parallel between glass and metal work, we see the wide employment of enamelled decorations in very bright colours against a dark background, generally deep blue, emerald-green or red. The decoration is produced by the system of vitrified colours fixed by reheating the object a second time. If the imitation of metalware is evident in the shapes of this glassware, it seems that its decoration too bears some relation to the art of enamelled ornamentation of metal, which was very fashionable in the 14th century and became even more so during the Renaissance, especially in France. In such glasses we find, in particular, the employment of dark backgrounds — dark blue or even black — with decorations in very bright colours, including gold, superimposed. It will be sufficient to mention the extremely rich range of glasses manufactured in Limoges up to the end of the 16th century. On the other hand it would not be difficult, by searching among literary and iconographic sources, to trace analogies of style and origin between the subjects represented by painters on glass and in contemporary miniature painting. In fact, the same cortèges are reproduced: the Triumphs of Bacchus or Venus, the Fountains of Love and also the various sacred scenes which ornamented liturgical vessels. We reproduce here the superb goblet decorated with a Fountain of Love, belonging to the Murano museum, which tradition attributes to the Barovier family of glass-makers. We may also observe the use of identical embellishments such as flourishes, wreaths, woven lines and scrolls resembling the initial letters or illuminated borders of parchments, sometimes combined with dedicatory portraits after the style of medallions, from which they are undoubtedly derived. It is also very interesting to note the frequent use of intensely dark backgrounds to make the painted decorations stand out with the greatest possible clarity; this might be connected with the tendency to imitate the widespread enamelled decoration on metal objects, but it might also have been an attempt to render the object more precious at a time when glass had not yet reached that perfection of purity and transparency that was to be obtained later. Moreover, the shapes themselves often left much to be desired in respect of beauty of lines and proportions.

Hence the predilection for tinted glass may be regarded as the chief characteristic of the first high-quality glass manufactured in Italy — a characteristic that might well be derived from the art of stained glass so much in vogue throughout the Gothic period and the early Renaissance. This high-quality glass was obviously a result of collaboration between glass-makers and miniature-painters. The art of miniature painting already had its own tradition which had developed in the shadow of

xxiii BOWL-SHAPED CHALICE WITH LID, INSPIRED BY METAL TYPES. VENETIAN (OR FRENCH?) ART OF THE 16TH CENTURY. PERUGIA, PRIVATE COLLECTION.

Western Gothic in the North, which included Venice, even though the latter was under the influence of more illustrious centres situated in nearby Romagna and particularly in Lombardy. Venice at this moment was looking towards the mainland, henceforth paying little tribute to Byzantine stylisation, which had already been abandoned in the figurative arts. We must not forget what was happening in the field of painting at the same period, round 1460-80, the date to which we believe the aforementioned goblets should be attributed. Nor must we overlook the new humanistic culture in which Venetian artists seem to have competed with the Paduans, just when the art of Andrea Mantegna, who exercised so much influence on the development of his brother-in-law Giovanni Bellini, was initiating and moulding the 'Vivarini manner' and the so-called 'School of Murano.' It was not by chance, therefore, that while Muranese paint-ers followed a path of absolute innovation — as the school of Mantegna represented at that time — other Muranese or possibly Ve-netian artists collaborated to bring further embellishment to the glasses that their col-league the glass-maker had blown for them. We need only observe the intense refinement of the portraits, for example, in the goblet belonging to the British Museum. Oddly enough, as the result, apparently, of these craftsmen's exaggerated modesty, not a single piece has come down to us bearing a signature, a seal or any other identification mark. Con-sequently it is virtually impossible to classify any pieces, even those of an exceptional char-acter, with accuracy. Some attempts have been made to trace the paternity of certain pieces, such as the goblet belonging to the Murano museum, which is now traditionally ascribed to the Baroviers, an attribution for which there is some evidence, although it is rather uncertain, since it is not based on spe-cific documents but on general references to the activities of Angelo Barovier and other master glass-blowers of his family, who were well known even beyond the boundaries of Venice during the Renaissance. Similarly, modern critics have fairly sound reasons for considering Antonio da Murano, alias Vivarini, to have been the author of the decorations on the Bolognese goblet bearing *The Flight into Egypt*. Antonio, whose activities date from around this period, was the son of a master *fiolario* and the brother of another Muranese painter, Bartolomeo Vivarini; the latter, to-gether with the Venetian Mocetto and in col-laboration with the glass-maker G. A. Licinio, executed the big stained-glass window of the church of Sts. John and Paul in Venice. In any case, certain inventions and refinements of colouration in glass-painting would be in-explicable except in terms of contacts with the major arts of the time. As a typical example, we may quote the glass decorated with sacred and allegoric scenes now housed in the Berlin museum.

Although the decorator sometimes displays a more ingenuous, or more simply popular style, we may nevertheless say that in general reflections of these major arts are never miss-ing. The sensibility and fervour of the new Renaissance world of which Venice, even though belatedly, became one of the main pillars in Italy, fully inform the minor arts and, above all, the art of glass-making. Mean-while technical progress led to the search for a more refined material. That is perhaps why, while pictorial external decoration continued to remain in favour, there was an increasingly decisive tendency towards transparency of the background. Certainly, as was the case with others already mentioned, this procedure was not without precedents. Chief among these were the famous hanging lamps for mosques having the typical shape of a vase with an extra-large base, provided with suspension rings, painted with polychrome enamels, and bearing inscriptions (verses from the Koran or dedications) and various decorative motifs. These lamps, characteristic of Syrian produc-tion during the 14th century, continued to be manufactured in the following century and later, and eventually spread to Venice itself. This very interesting fact is proved by diplo-matic documents relating to orders for such lamps from Muranese workshops, at the height of the 16th century, to be made from designs supplied by the customer. Whether we explain this new development mainly or partially by the foregoing facts, or by the emergence of new aesthetic demands within the field of Venetian glass-making, there can be no doubt that at the end of the 15th and the beginning of the 16th century transparent glass with enamelled dec-orations, similar to what had gone before but more restricted in range, became prevalent. The colours are very vivid — red, emerald-green, blue, white; the motifs are taken from natural subjects, including branches, bunches of grapes and vine leaves, ribbons, knotted cords, flowers, especially lilies of the valley (the art of the miniature still exercised a dominant influence on glass decoration).

xxiv

xxv

xxvi

xxvii

xxiv BOWL-SHAPED GOBLET WITH DECORATIONS APPLIED TO THE STEM (IN IMITATION OF THE VENETIAN STYLE). FLORENTINE WORKSHOP (EARLY 17TH CENTURY). FLORENCE, MUSEO DI STORIA DELLA SCIENZA. *xxv* CURIOUSLY SHAPED VASE ('ZUCCARIN') INSPIRED BY 'GUTTROLF' GERMAN TYPES. MURANESE WORKSHOP (LATE 16TH CENTURY). MURANO, MUSEO VETRARIO. *xxvi* WINGED GOBLET. VENETIAN ART OR 'FAÇON DE VENI-SE' (LATE 16TH CENTURY). MURANO, MUSEO VETRARIO. *xxvii* BOTTLE OF THE 'PERRON' TYPE. SPANISH ART (16TH OR 17TH CENTURY). BARCE-LONA, MUSEO DE ARTES DECORATIVAS.

xxviii CHALICE WITH STEM DECORATED WITH WINGS OR 'SERPENTS' IN THE VENETIAN MANNER. FLORENTINE WORKSHOP (17TH CENTURY). FORMERLY IN THE ACCADEMIA DEL CIMENTO, NOW IN FLORENCE, MUSEO DI STORIA DELLA SCIENZA.

xxix ORNAMENTAL VASE WITH THREE SPOUTS DECORATED WITH FLOWERS AND FLOURISHES, IMITATION OF THE VENETIAN MANNER. FLORENTINE WORKSHOP (17TH CENTURY). FORMERLY IN THE ACCADEMIA DEL CIMENTO, NOW IN FLORENCE, MUSEO DI STORIA DELLA SCIENZA.

XXX TWO-HANDLED VASE WITH LID, OF FROSTED GLASS, IMITATION OF THE VENETIAN MANNER. FLORENTINE WORKSHOP (17TH CENTURY). FORMERLY IN THE ACCADEMIA DEL CIMENTO, NOW IN FLORENCE, MUSEO DI STORIA DELLA SCIENZA.

Very often the enamel decoration is made up of numerous dots set out in parallel lines or arranged on the pattern of scales, a method of ornamentation typical of this period and attested by many examples. The objects did not change greatly in shape; we still find chalices, goblets with funnel-shaped bases and prominent ribs, with or without a knot, frequently reminiscent of metal vessels in shape. Indeed, in certain categories of objects the

derivation is even more surprisingly direct. We find cylindrical reliquaries, like those of gold or silver, with a base and a lid surmounted by a small cross, low flat pyxes with a lid

and worked with an embossed lozenge pattern, jugs with a handle and smooth flat base, and finally hanging lamps to light the sacred chapels, which, because of their cylindrical shape running to a point and terminated by a drop, have retained the name *cesendelli* originally applied to silver or bronze lamps. These are examples of great interest, typifying a particular style in vogue around the beginning of the 16th century, to be seen in paintings of the period and in a specimen of great rarity displayed in the Murano museum. We often find in the glasses of the same era a raised pattern which we might call embossed to emphasize its derivation from metal work. To the motifs which henceforth inspired painters on glass, we may now add heraldic decorations, such as the coats of arms of the Sforzas and of the Bentivoglios which ornament the two flasks belonging to the Bologna museum — two of the very few specimens of which the actual date is known, because of the reference to the wedding between two members of these families in 1492 — and the coat of arms of

the Sforzas in a chalice included in the collection in the Castello Sforzesco, Milan; and finally the coats of arms of the Tiepolos and the Barbarigos, to be seen respectively on a *cesendello* and on a plate exhibited in the Murano museum — the latter also dating from the end of the 15th century. The shape of the Sforzesco chalice, too, is reminiscent of

those metal objects whose shapes had already

been imitated for some time in glassware of the commonest types used on the dinner tables of the Gothic period. We find very clear examples portrayed in figurative art from the 14th century mosaics in St. Mark's down to the mosaics in Pomposa and later works.

FIG. xii

The 16th century seems therefore to begin with a new aim in the minds of the Muranese glass-blowers: to reduce or entirely eliminate applied pictorial decoration in order thereby to give full value to the material itself. Technical progress permitted the manufacture of a purer, more limpid and lighter glass, which was at the same time more subtle and precise in shape. As for colour, it is still sometimes

used, but it is incorporated in the material itself, the glass being of one colour, either red, pale blue or violet. As has been mentioned, the Romans already produced glass tinted in a single colour, thus anticipating the Venetians

even in this field. On the other hand, one of the newest and most characteristic types of Renaissance glass was 'chalcedony', the devel-

opment of which may be attributed to the naturalistic and scientific tendencies inherent in the cultural outlook of the Renaissance. Chalcedony glass, which took its name from the stone by which it was inspired, was employed for objects of any shape and presented a variegated surface of different colours; the objects vary greatly in size and include quite large articles such as plates, jugs and ampulae provided with a small spout.

We may also remind the reader of another type of glass manufactured by the Romans, with applied decorations consisting of thin white threads. Muranese glass-blowers revived this technique and even found means of incor-

porating the milky-white threads in the object while it was still hot, thus fusing them with the generally transparent material out of which the vessels were blown. This type of glass came to be called *lattimo*, from *latte* meaning milk. The result of this procedure was a series of parallel vertical stripes, sometimes close together, sometimes further apart, and varying in other ways according to the particular design. Sometimes white stripes alternate with coloured ones. These white threads, arranged in a spiral and interlacing pattern, create a delightfully delicate effect in contrast with the transparency of the main body of the vessel. This system produced the *reticelli*, or reticulated glasses, decorated with single or double threads, or alternate canes, and finally stripes so close together as entirely to cover the object, creating an extremely attractive effect. A few museums, particularly that at Murano, house specimens of this kind, including some remarkably large round plates, which indicate the skill and experience which master glass-blowers had by now acquired; there are also cups and drinking glasses, round double-handled basins with a lid called *ciste*, trays with a base, bottles and perfume flasks, fruit dishes, such as the one shown in Pl. 47, belonging to the Turin museum, and a rich variety of other pieces now housed in collections in Turin, Paris, London, Vienna and so on. Fashionable throughout the height of the 16th century, *reticello* glass, also called 'filigree' because of its resemblance to goldsmiths' work, was not always all white; sometimes threads of different colours, chiefly red and blue, were added in interlacing or parallel stripes forming very lovely patterns.

PLS. 43-48

As for pictorial decoration, colour was almost completely abandoned, at least so far as enamelled decorations were concerned. Especially round the middle of the 16th century enamelling was replaced by the more expeditious *a freddo* method of painting on the object when cool without reheating it. This system did not require the painter to go to work immediately the object emerged from the furnace; indeed, he could carry out his decorations a long time after the object had been produced, since he merely had to paint on the cold surface, in particular the underside of the bases of glasses, plates, goblets and of those cups which had a base. The artists drew their inspiration from fashionable subjects, finding a direct and virtually inexhaustible source of inspiration in prints and wood engravings, which had become widely distributed since the beginning of the century. As in the preceding period, the art of the miniature had influenced glass-painting, so now a similar influence was exercised by the art of book illustration and decoration, from which glass-painters took mythological or allegorical scenes, portraits and landscapes. Naturally, too, ideas were taken from individual prints, from which even great painters did not disdain to draw inspiration. Examples of this are the well known prints by Marco Antonio Raimondi. We shall therefore not be surprised to find glass decorators imitating, with little or no change, subjects like *Raphael's Dream*, which appears on a plate exhibited in the Murano museum, or the *Judgment of Paris* to be seen on a similar plate at Turin. Even Giorgione drew inspiration from Raimondi's print, *Raphael's Dream*, for a Venus which has now unfortunately disappeared. It would be interesting and revealing to investigate the sources of painted decorations, in a similar manner to that which has been suggested for enamelled decorations. Certainly the result would once more confirm the link between the major and so-called minor arts during the fervent Humanistic period. The creative eagerness that characterised the 16th century was also manifest in the art of glass-making; it was a period of research and striving after innovation, as can be inferred from entirely new forms whose perfection rivalled that of the works of antiquity. We cannot rule out the possible direct or indirect intervention of the great artists who led Venice at that glorious historical moment into the realm of the Muses. The elegance and exquisite refinement of some objects, and even the strange preciosity of others — table-lamps shaped like little horses or mice, water jugs like tiny galleys with open-work sails — can only be explained by close contact with current trends in pictorial art. It is not without reason that the name of Armenia Vivarini has been associated by critics with the glass galleys.

She was the daughter of the painter Alvise Vi-

PL.

PL.

PL.

PL.

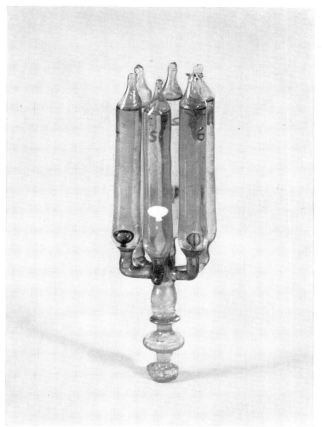

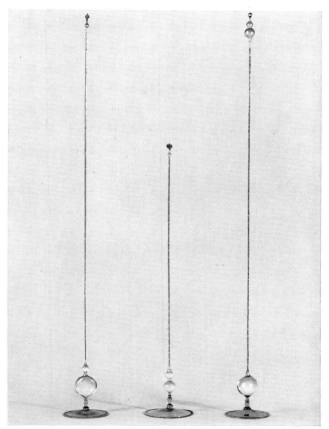

xxxi

xxxii

xxxi THERMOMETER WITH SIX ELEMENTS, FLORENTINE WORKSHOP (17TH CENTURY). FORMERLY IN THE ACCADEMIA DEL CIMENTO, NOW IN FLORENCE, MUSEO DI STORIA DELLA SCIENZA.

xxxii THREE ALCOHOL THERMOMETERS WITH LONG ROD. FLORENTINE WORKSHOP (17TH CENTURY). FORMERLY IN THE ACCADEMIA DEL CIMENTO, NOW IN FLORENCE, MUSEO DI STORIA DELLA SCIENZA.

xxxiii SPIRAL THERMOMETER. FLORENTINE WORKSHOP (17TH CENTURY). FORMERLY IN THE ACCADEMIA DEL CIMENTO, NOW IN FLORENCE, MUSEO DI STORIA DELLA SCIENZA.

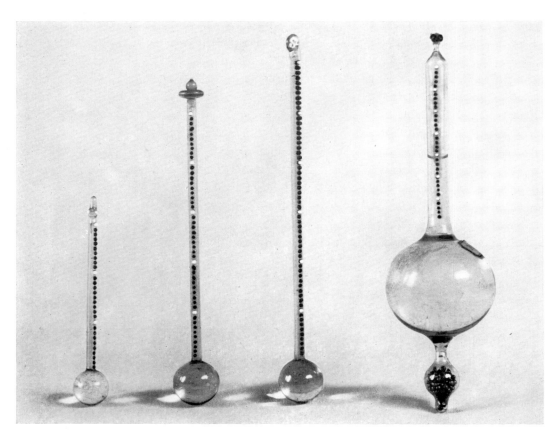

xxxiv FOUR ALCOHOL THERMOMETERS WITH VERTICAL ROD. FLORENTINE WORKSHOP (17TH CENTURY). FORMERLY IN THE ACCADEMIA DEL CIMENTO, NOW IN FLORENCE, MUSEO DI STORIA DELLA SCIENZA. *xxxv* GROUP OF SPIRAL AND ALCOHOL THERMOMETERS. FLORENTINE WORKSHOP (17TH CENTURY). FORMERLY IN THE ACCADEMIA DEL CIMENTO, NOW IN FLORENCE, MUSEO DI STORIA DELLA SCIENZA.

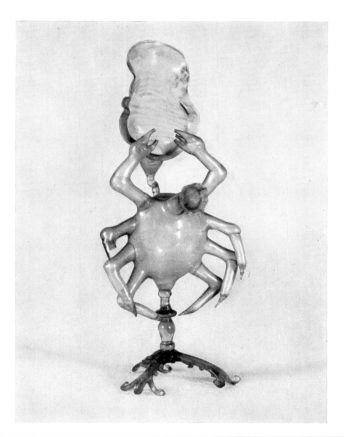

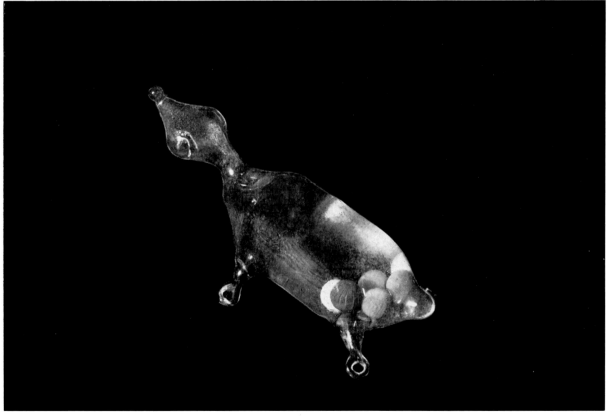

xxxvi TABLE LAMP IN THE SHAPE OF A CRAB. FLORENTINE WORKSHOP (17TH CENTURY). FORMERLY IN THE ACCADEMIA DEL CIMENTO, NOW IN FLORENCE, MUSEO DI STORIA DELLA SCIENZA. *xxxvii* CLINICAL THERMOMETER IN THE SHAPE OF A FROG OR TOAD. FLORENTINE WORKSHOP (17TH CENTURY). FORMERLY IN THE ACCADEMIA DEL CIMENTO, NOW IN FLORENCE, MUSEO DI STORIA DELLA SCIENZA.

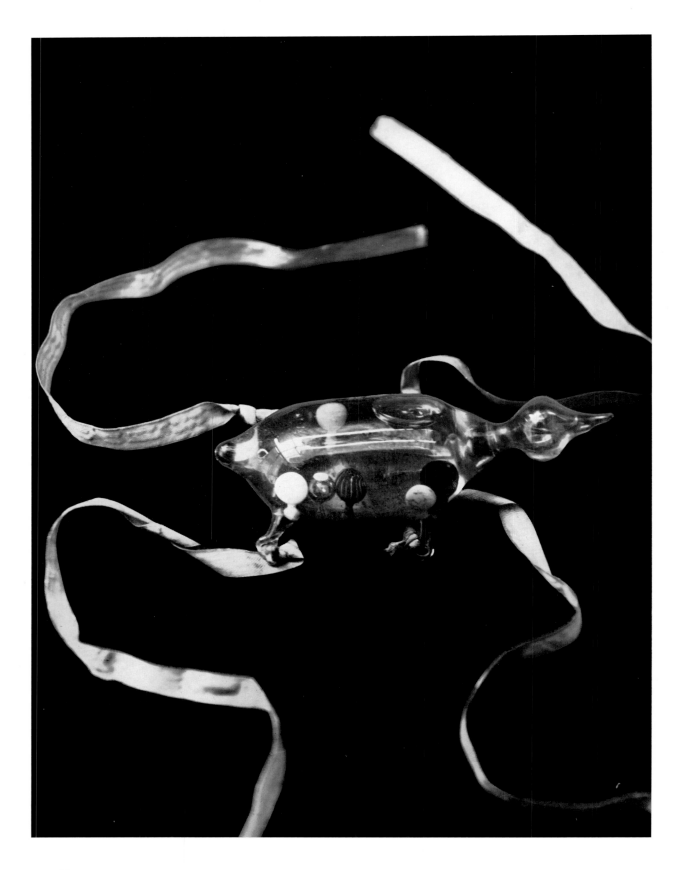

xxxviii CLINICAL THERMOMETER IN THE SHAPE OF A FROG OR TOAD, WITH RIBBONS TO ATTACH IT TO THE PATIENT'S ARM. FLORENTINE WORK-SHOP (17TH CENTURY). FORMERLY IN THE ACCADEMIA DEL CIMENTO, NOW IN FLORENCE, MUSEO DI STORIA DELLA SCIENZA.

varini and possibly a painter herself — although there is no documentary evidence of this — active in Murano during the second half of the 16th century. And who would deny in principle that even the greatest names of the Italian Renaissance — from Paolo Veronese to Tintoretto, from Palma il Giovane to Jacopo da Bassano — might on some occasions have assisted the glass-maker to evolve new forms, if only by providing him with sketches or drawings. Aretino in his *Letters* bears witness to one of them, the painter Giovanni da Udine, having done this. If we disregard literary references to objects of quite ordinary shapes, and the numerous pictures by the artists we have mentioned in which such glass vessels are portrayed — we need only think of the *Suppers* by Veronese or Tintoretto and others — we must not overlook the great attention paid to the proportions, the subtle elegance of the outline, the harmony between the parts evident in objects produced at this period, in conformity with the laws of classical architecture then dominant. The absence of colour in many of the Muranese products of this period — although apparently strange in the very century in which Venice gained her hegemony in the field of painting — is chiefly to be explained by the tendency towards that perfection and harmony of forms which glass-makers were undoubtedly striving after. They were also confirmed in this trend by the development which represents their major achievement, the invention for which they were to become world-famous, namely colourless glass itself, which they themselves called 'crystal' and which was obtained at the beginning of the 16th century with the aid of a special formula and a careful process of decoloration. We refer here to objects of the purest character, that is to say free from any pictorial decoration. Strictly speaking, clear glass or, as it was then called, 'crystalline' glass, already existed in the second half of the 14th century, but it was then still inseparable from pictorial decorations.

In his *Trattato d'Architettura*, Filarete men-

tions these glasses with admiration and we know that they were exhibited and appreciated in the great Ascension Fair in St. Mark's Square. The superiority of crystalline glass over the more usual and common articles, rightly considered inferior, was confirmed by the severe regulations controlling retail sales. In particular, peddlers and *stazioneri* or stall-holders were excluded, because the best pieces were sold directly by the producers in their shops situated in the town centre. One of these shops standing next to the Sansovinian Library on St. Mark's jetty, with its windows showing glasses of every possible type, is clearly depicted in a contemporary print by Josse Amman of Zurich. It must be remembered that Muranese crystalline glass, even if it is much clearer than earlier glass, bears no relation to crystal proper, which is based on lead or potassium oxides and was created two centuries later in England and Bohemia. The difference is clearly visible in the material itself: extremely limpid but cold in the case of 18th century European crystal, slightly yellowish and sometimes *fumé* in the case of Muranese crystalline glass which is still based on the old compounds, lime and soda, with the addition of decolorants. The major achievement involved in this new Venetian invention was rather the perfection of the shapes coupled with the abandonment of any mechanical instrument. In Muranese glass workshops, the work was carried out solely with the aid of a few indispensable tools in addition to the traditional blowpipe, or at most the possible use of a mould to obtain certain predetermined effects. A particular category of objects was created, recognizable by their surface covered by a regular relief pattern obtained by incision — sometimes small bosses, sometimes lozenges or rhombs — that enveloped cups, vases and drinking glasses like an invisible net. This technique which, according to recent investigations (Gasparetto, 1951), reveals contacts and exchanges with German art in addition to the clear connections with the late Gothic style, also dates from the previous century. Moulds were usually also

xxxix WATER BOWL AND SAUCER OF MILK-GLASS, FROM "BACCHUS AS A BOY" BY GUIDO RENI (17TH CENTURY). FLORENCE, GALLERIA PITTI.

employed for shaping the stems of chalices decorated with masks, festoons or lions' heads, in lively contrast with the linear simplicity of the bowl of the glass. In some cases glass was pressed into moulds reproducing figures of an iconographic type, obviously taken from contemporary plaques or medals. Finally, it should be remembered that the only element of colour tolerated in Muranese 'crystal' glass was azure or aquamarine decorations, consisting of thin coloured lines running along the borders, stems or handles; out of these developed the small wings and the complicated open-work ornamentations so dear to the Baroque era.

The first half of the 16th century represents the heyday of Muranese production; it was a real golden age as regards quality and refinement, not only in the manufacture of exceptional objects, but also in that of everyday ware, as is proved by paintings of the period. In fact the traditional and still common drink-ing glasses, shaped like a truncated cone, and with no base, painted by Crivelli or Marco da Marziale, lead on to the spherical bottles with a long neck, to the chalices with a low base, to the elongated goblets and round bowls, to the jugs with curved spout and handle as in those made of metal — objects often to be seen in paintings by Bonifacio, Tintoretto, Leandro Bassano, Paris Bordone, Veronese and other artists after them, down to the end of the 16th century. Concrete evidence of all this is provided by the varied collections in certain museums, including, of course, that at Murano. Here we may see not only table-ware such as beakers and extremely refined chalices with the stem shaped like a small column or balustrade — reminiscent of the Palladian style — but also vials for liturgical use. ornamental vases, dishes and cylindrical reliquaries with a lid surmounted by a small cross, certainly imitated from commoner types in metal. Such

38

xl

xli

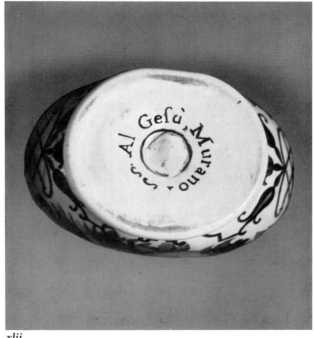

xlii

xl MUG AND SAUCER OF MILK-GLASS DECORATED WITH LANDSCAPE MOTIFS. VENETIAN ART (18TH CENTURY). LONDON, VICTORIA AND ALBERT MUSEUM.
xli TRADE MARK OF THE MIOTTI WORKSHOP OF MURANO (18TH CENTURY). MURANO, MUSEO VETRARIO. *xlii* 'AL GESÙ, MURANO': MARK AND SIGN
OF THE MIOTTI WORKSHOP ON THE BASE OF A SMALL BOTTLE OF PAINTED MILK-GLASS (18TH CENTURY). MURANO, MUSEO VETRARIO.

xliii TWO MILK-GLASS VASES. VENETIAN ART (18TH CENTURY). VENICE, CA' REZZONICO.

objects, which combined incomparable elegance of line with the attraction of an astonishing transparency and purity, could not fail to be greatly admired and sought after. This was in fact the moment of maximum expansion for the Venetian glass-makers, who not only exported widely to foreign countries and to the courts and nobility of Italy and Europe, but also began to yield to that migratory movement which, on the one hand did credit to the ability and skill of Italian craftsmen, and on the other presented serious dangers. Well aware of these, the Republic had imposed extremely severe penalties on emigration; nevertheless, it did not succeed in preventing master craftsmen from leaving and taking with them technical secrets, methods and styles, as a result of which Venice gradually lost the advantages of her previous monopoly.

At this point we must recall that, partly through its own fault, Murano was no longer alone in Europe. Even in Italy itself other centres of the glass-making industry had emerged. For some time already workshops had been active in the Venetian cities of Padua, Treviso, Vicenza, Verona and, farther away, in Brescia and Bergamo, and also in Ferrara, Ravenna, Bologna and Ancona. In Liguria, especially, apparently from the beginning of the 11th century, glass-making flourished in the industrious village of Altare. The Altarese masters, who were undoubtedly in touch with those from Venice — Altare was one of the many places to which Venetian masters emigrated — helped to speed up that process of expansion which Venice, in spite of having assisted it commercially, now tried to block in response to the pressing needs of protectionism. Not being bound by the chains that made emigration difficult for the Muranese, the glass-makers of Altare freely went abroad, in particular to nearby France, taking with them the forms of taste and the stylistic elements of the art and facilitating the establishment of the various centres in Provence, Lorraine, Normandy, and Belgium. Although indirectly, the spread of glass-making from

xliv PAINTED MILK-GLASS JAR WITH LID, PORCELAIN TYPE. VENETIAN ART (18TH CENTURY). LONDON, VICTORIA AND ALBERT MUSEUM.

xlv SMALL, EXTREMELY THIN MILK-GLASS CUP WITH TWO HANDLES, EACH COMPOSED OF A DOUBLE TENDRIL. VENETIAN ART (LATE 18TH CENTURY). PERUGIA, PRIVATE COLLECTION.

FIGS. xvi, xxvii

Murano also reached Spain, where the Renaissance brought about a fashion for enamelled glass produced in the region of Barcelona, while from the 15th to the end of the 16th century the same type of ware was exported to Austria and Germany. In the meantime, European countries displayed a tendency to develop a local style, although it was still based on the example of the highly skilled Muranese. During the 16th century, Flanders saw the birth of an industry fed by commercial contacts and even more by the flow of migration from Italy, and more particularly through the influx of the glass-makers from Altare, which was now dominated by the 'Università dell'Arte Vitrea,' that is to say by a highly organised corporation governed by a Council and codified in 1495 in a systematic and definitive statute, which seems to have been created especially to foster and develop these fruitful contacts. The popularity and imitation of the imported specimens favoured the development of the so-called *façon de Venise*, the expression of a current of sympathy which, however, soon led to independent local activity. Meanwhile the Venetian emigration had spread everywhere — including Holland, Sweden, Denmark and Britain. The diffusion of forms learned and imitated from those of Murano reached such proportions at one time that it is occasionally difficult to distinguish the objects which originated from the glass-houses of the Lagoon from the copies made beyond the Alps. The difficulty is intensified by the fact that, at least in the early stages, these articles were often the handiwork of expatriate Muranese craftsmen. A great many names, some of them belonging to the most famous glass-making families of Murano, are recorded in documents or other written sources as having worked in the various countries, thus fostering the development of an industry which was destined one day to offer formidable competition to that of Venice.

PLS. 55-57

Meanwhile, shapes evolved and changed in Venice itself. Certain decorative elements introduced into the primitive structure of the object, which was first simply and purely organic, tended little by little to modify it. Examples of this process are the well known 'wings' added to the stem of goblets — small FIG scrolls decorated with crests, open-work and pointed projections, forming graceful and charming arabesques, which became increasingly complex in response to a taste which undoubtedly matured outside Italy: it is no coincidence that this type of vessel made a triumphant entry into the Northern repertory of the *façon de Venise*.

At a certain point the technical means became an end in themselves and this fact, as always happens in art, marked the beginning of decline, the disruption of Renaissance balance, the exhaustion of vital inspiration. The golden age of the 16th century came to an end and the beginning of the 17th brought the increasingly categorical advance of the Baroque style, which was able to exploit the new fashion for complex decorations, employed especially to add even greater richness to luxury objects. Although we do not know precisely when or by whom the technique of incising with a diamond or flint point was PLS introduced, it may be deduced that it was already in full swing by the middle of the 16th century. Incisions were very light, no more than scratches — the light, thin glass would not have stood up to deeper cuts. The motifs are very simple, rarely figurative, most often taken from the plant world (branches, sprays of leaves, tendrils, etc.), sometimes covering the whole surface of the object. We rarely encounter pieces with dedicatory inscriptions, names and dates. As we have already noted, the most absolute anonymity is typical of Venetian glass, and it is only thanks to documents and the lists of the *Mariegole* (or statutes of the art of glass-making) that a few names have come down to us. Contrary to what happened in other countries such as Flanders or Bohemia, no Venetian master glass-maker was in the habit of signing or sealing his own work. The gracefulness of the decorations incised on Italian glassware during

xlvi BEAKER WITH THE DOGAL ARMS OF THE MOCENIGOS. VENETIAN ART (18TH CENTURY). MURANO, MUSEO VETRARIO.

xlvii CHANDELIER WITH A GLOBE AND TWO SUPERIMPOSED SETS OF ARMS OF WHITE GLASS. FROM THE BRIATI FACTORY (?) (18TH CENTURY). VENICE, CA' REZZONICO.

xlviii

xlix

xlviii SMALL POLYGONAL VOTIVE BOTTLE BEARING THE IMAGE OF ST NICHOLAS (18TH CENTURY). PERUGIA, PRIVATE COLLECTION. *xlix* PHARMACEUTI-
CAL GLASS JAR DECORATED 'A FREDDO' WITH PLANT MOTIFS AND LETTERING. VENETIAN ART (18TH CENTURY). VENICE, SALVIATI-CAMERINO COLLECTION.
l LIDDED JAR OF STAMPED GLASS AND BEAKER PAINTED WITH WHITE ENAMEL DEPICTING 'REBECCA AT THE WELL'. VENETIAN ART (18TH CENTURY).
FORMERLY FORTUNY COLLECTION, NOW AT MURANO, MUSEO VETRARIO.

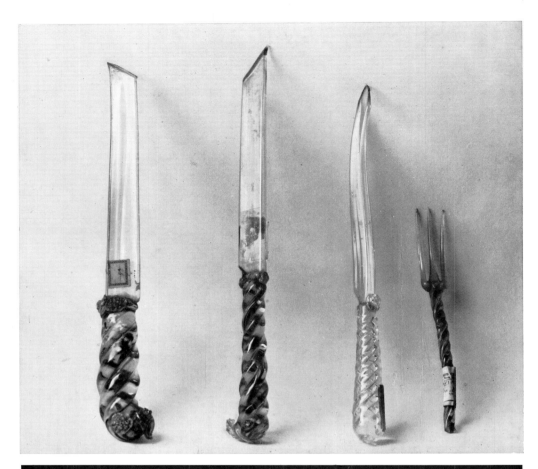

li KNIVES AND FORK OF WHITE AND COLOURED GLASS. VENETIAN ART (18TH CENTURY). MURANO, MUSEO VETRARIO.
lii GOBLETS CONTAINING MEDAL: THAT ON THE LEFT BEARS THE NAME OF THE LAST DOGE, LUDOVICO MANIN, AND THE DATE 1796. MURANO, MUSEO VETRARIO.

the second half of the 16th century and in the 17th century bears witness to the favour which this technique also enjoyed in Venice, although it must be admitted that it never attained the extreme refinement of Dutch glass. Frosted glass with a wrinkled surface ornamented with masks and other externally applied decorations also enjoyed great success.

We must now consider another branch of the art which began in Venice during the 16th century and rapidly acquired international fame. This is the art of the mirror, a branch in which the Venetians attained a special position, almost a monopoly, for a long time. It is well known that even during the Middle Ages, as had been the case in antiquity, mirrors were made of metal, especially silver, highly polished on one face and gracefully decorated on the other. We do not know exactly when glass first came to be employed in place of metal. It would seem almost certain, however, though it originated in Germany, that the Venetians were certainly among the first to spread the manufacture and use of glass mirrors between the end of the 15th and the beginning of the 16th century. Moreover, they brought them to the highest pitch of perfection, creating around the mirror, which was usually quadrangular in shape, a frame that was itself made of glass held together by metal connections. The frame, and very often the actual surface of the mirror contained within it, bore incised or ground decorations cut into facets, or floral and figurative patterns executed by a technique which reached its heyday in the 18th century in Venice; although, under the guide of the astute Colbert, the French were already organising an industry of their own in the 17th century.

We cannot say much about the other Italian glass-making centres during this period, because Murano was undoubtedly far ahead of all the rest and gained a monopoly in certain particular branches of manufacture, among which, as we have just seen, was the production of mirrors and, in general, of luxury articles. We have already spoken of Altare, perhaps the major centre after Murano. It is to be assumed that in the other places in Italy where there was a glass-making industry, it was devoted not so much to objects of art as to simpler or more commonplace vessels intended for everyday use. This does not mean, of course, that the Muranese workshops did not also produce objects of inferior quality to satisfy local, and so far as possible, foreign demands. We must remember, among other things, window-panes, table-ware, and finally the felicitous activity of the bead-makers with their beads, heated on an open flame (*a lume*), which were used primarily for personal adornment. Solid evidence of this trade in utilitarian glassware is provided by the existence of inventories and documents of considerable interest to anyone wishing to study the economic and industrial situation at that time.

We shall now consider Tuscany in connection with a very special product within the field of utilitarian ware. At Empoli, Pisa, Lucca and Florence itself there were blown the famous *fiasche* or bulb-shaped glass bottles encased in straw which served, then as now, for carrying small quantities of wine as well as water and other beverages. Various types of such bottles came from these workshops during the 16th century and later, and were widely exported; there is also documentary evidence, from the 14th century onwards, of the manufacture of table glasses, a line of production subsequently increased by the establishment of numerous workshops devoted to the production of glass beakers. As regards high-quality glass on the other hand, the Tuscans lacked the equipment and the master glass-makers capable of competing with the Venetians, in spite of some attempts, encouraged by the Grand Dukes during the 16th century, to manufacture objects similar to those produced by the Muranese: goblets with winged stems, bowls, cups, etc., a few examples of which have come down to us, whose place of origin is not easily determined and which are described as being *alla veneziana*,

61

FIG. XX

FIGS. *xxiii, xxix*

47

'in the Venetian manner'. The Florentine masters devoted themselves more successfully, during the 16th and 17th centuries, to a more technical or — as we should say today — scientific group of objects: glasses for medicinal or pharmaceutical use. It was no coincidence that Tuscany, the fatherland of Galileo, was also the cradle of researches anticipating many of the achievements of the modern era — as a typical example let us recall the thermometer. Hence it is not surprising that, to satisfy the demands of the 16th century scientific investigators and alchemists, the glass workshops should have specialised in this very particular field, producing retorts, alembics, small pots, vials, and objects especially adapted to the most various requirements. The St. Geminiano museum and the museum of the History of Science in Florence (containing the glasses of the famous and admirable Accademia del Cimento) include among their possessions a copious collection of such pieces in a wide and curious variety of forms and types. Naturally enough, 'scientific' glasses were also manufactured in the workshops of the Venetian Lagoon. We need only recall the work done in this field by a master glass-maker who had his workshop in Murano in the second half of the 16th century — Niccolò dell'Aquila, who was so much praised by his contemporary Fioravanti. He devoted himself in particular to the manufacture of decanters and alembics, as well as special lanterns of his own invention. During the Renaissance other types of glasses were also manufactured in Venice for medical and alchemistic use, such as the glass boilers and the jars for distilling alcohol referred to by Bringuccio in his *Pirotecnia* (printed in 1540), and even excellent clepsydras, consisting of two spheres one above the other. However, the most important production did not come into being until later, in the 18th century, with the development of pharmaceutical glass vessels. It is interesting to recall that Galileo, who was in contact with the Serenissima Repubblica, and during a stay in Padua devoted himself to the study of the

manufacture of telescope lenses, made use, at least to begin with, of equipment produced in Murano — equipment which he had sent to him from the Lagoon even after his return to his own country, as is attested by documentary evidence. Moreover, among other activities of the Muranese, there are records of true spectacles, which were in use in Veneto (as may be seen from certain pictorial representations — for example, the frescoes of Tommaso da Modena at Treviso) from the 14th century onwards. The craft of spectacle-making, which flourished in the 17th century, was certainly carried on in active contact and interchange with Florentine manufacturers and opticians.

Among the various types of bottles and flasks produced in Tuscany, we must recall the original *cantinflora* celebrated by Redi: a bottle with a long curved spout and inner receptacle — also of glass — to contain ice, a very practical invention, even now sometimes to be seen on modern tables. The 17th century was the period of maximum expansion for Tuscany and the local industry. We have documentary evidence of many workshops devoted to the manufacture of *fiaschi*, especially in Florence itself and in the localities of Prato, Figline Valdarno, Fucecchio, and Montepulciano; beaker-makers worked at Arezzo, San Miniato, Pistoia, Pescia and Cortona, and also at Empoli, Montelupo and Borgo San Lorenzo. Severe and wise legislation protected glass-making, as it did the other industries within the territories of the Signoria. The activities of glass-makers also came under the control of the Craft Guilds, although both the beaker-makers and glass-makers in general were combined with other crafts, especially those of the Physicians and Druggists, having no guild of their own. That the industry had progressed technically in the 17th century in Tuscany is also proved by the publication of the most important treatise of its kind, Antonio Neri's *Arte Vetraria*, which was printed in Florence in 1612 and re-issued in several successful editions. It must be noted that, as he tells us himself, Neri, a Florentine abbot, had personal experience in glass-making, and that the aim of his book was to sum up all the results of the technical and scientific progress achieved by scholars and craftsmen whom he had approached, well aware how much the craft owed to these experimenters, who were the new heirs of the ancient alchemists, and to the illustrious Maecenases of his city. It was not for nothing that he dedicated his treatise to the Grand Duke Antonio de' Medici, himself an ardent scholar and the enlightened protector of scientists and artists. Before leaving Tuscany we have still to recall that the art of painted glass windows was much prized here, which encouraged the manufacture of glass plates for this purpose; if at one time they were of necessity imported from Germany or from Venice, they were cut and painted on the spot, and special furnaces and crucibles were employed for the process of reheating which followed the painting. Finally, with the last of the Medici and as the 18th century drew to a close, the art of glass-making in Tuscany fell into decline.

Let us then return to Venice, where, on the other hand, the production of artistic ware was expanding quantitatively in a positively alarming manner. Also in the art of glass, the 17th century had been characterised by the typical aspirations of every Baroque phase: an over-emphatic richness and variety of forms designed to astonish, and the desire to create curiosities that were often of an extravagant and fantastic nature. Sculptural decorations predominated, that is to say decorations moulded apart from the vessel itself, made of different colours and applied subsequently to the outer surface of the glass. At the same time, glass-makers continued to employ traditional decorations such as stamped masks, aquamarine twisted threads and the wings with which they enriched the stems of goblets. This system (to which we have already referred in connection with the *façon de Venise*) influenced by Flemish taste, reached its artistic and technical zenith at the end of the century. It seems as though glass-makers wished to offset

the absence of colour by straining after new, violently distorted, strange shapes that were more artificial than ever before. We find curious evidence of this chasing after eccentricity among the pages of a document which is of great importance to the history of glass-making: the *Libro del Principe Luigi d'Este*, which is preserved in the State Archives of Venice and constitutes a positive inventory of all the strange things produced by the glass-makers of Murano during the first half of the 17th century. In more than a thousand drawings it shows us a succession of strange small vases, flasks, lamps and mysterious vessels with their bodies shaped like birds, crabs, snails, lobsters and other fantastic animals, and even grotesque human figures, almost rivalling the works of contemporary sculptors. Objects of this nature may still be seen in certain collections (apart from that at Murano, in the Museo Poldi Pezzoli, in Milan); many of them are perplexingly strange and their original purpose is difficult to guess.

The phenomenon that accompanies the whole production of the 17th century was carried over to the following century but ran parallel with increased output. Murano now passed through a period of great prosperity, enjoying a fervour of productive activity not only in the field of glass-making but also in other branches of industry, such as pottery, furniture and silver-ware. The Venetian Guilds had never been so active, had never had under their control so many workshops and so many highly skilled master craftsmen. Not only the increased output but the great variety of techniques employed at this period confirms this. Apart from goblets, they made carafes and bottles of the most varied shapes, freely modelled or fashioned with moulds, which were increasingly used. Along with the usual everyday pieces which we see depicted in contemporary paintings (just as in previous centuries), we may observe in the 18th century a return to types and styles already successfully tried out in the past. Convincing evidence of the diffusion of Venetian glass abroad at the

FIG. xxxix

PLS. 55-57

xvi

49

beginning of the century may be seen in the purchases made at Murano by an illustrious personage of fine taste and culture, King Frederick the IV of Denmark, who ordered for his collection a noteworthy group of assorted objects which reached the royal residence of Rosenborg Castle in 1709. These objects, which are still in an excellent state of preservation, give us an idea of Muranese versatility, as evinced either in the repetition of previous shapes and techniques (frosted glass, reticulated glass, very thin blown glass in the shapes dear to the golden age), or by the adoption of the latest novelties, as is shown by certain bowl-shaped cups and goblets bearing decorations cut with the wheel, without doubt the first experiments in this technique to come from the hands of Venetian craftsmen.

FIGS. *xliii-xlv*

One of the techniques revived at this period was that of *lattimo* or milk-glass with its characteristic milky-white colour; the material thus obtained was exceptionally well suited to the imitation of porcelain, which the Venetians had at one time imported from the Far East and which, in Europe, only the Germans were now able to manufacture by means of secret processes discovered by themselves, although these processes were later also mastered by the Venetians. Thus we see extremely graceful cups and saucers, flasks and a lively assortment of other objects emerging from the Murano workshops. The background colour, which perfectly imitated the hue of porcelain, was combined with polychrome enamel decorations or more infrequently decorations painted *a freddo*, on the cold surface without reheating. The motifs, too, repeat those habitual to china objects, such as bunches of flowers, twigs, *chinoiseries* in very bright colours, including gold, birds, animals, and even small landscapes with figures in red like the typical 'sanguines' to be seen on the china cups of the Vezzi and the Cozzi. We may suppose that the success of this false porcelain (it was actually called 'counterfeit porcelain') was very considerable, since it continued to be produced even after the spread and manufacture of true porcelain.

FIG. *xl*

PLS. 62-66

FIG. *xliv*

Moreover, perhaps in imitation of the porcelain originals, milk-glass offers us the rare opportunity of learning the names of the artists in Murano who manufactured such objects, through the seals and trade-marks stamped upon them. We thus know that excellent work was done by the Miotti family, about whom we also have documentary information. They had a workshop on the island under the sign of 'Al Gesù' and in fact their trade-mark consisted of the seal IHS, standing for 'Jesus.' Some dated pieces show that the Miottis were active during the second half of the century, especially after 1770. Other Muranese well known for this particular activity were the Bertolinis, who taught the Miottis and achieved fame during the first decades of the 18th century. In the rich and varied collection of the local museum we find very graceful objects, many of which might be confused at first sight with the porcelains of the period. Many of them — such as the rare snuff-box in the shape of a flask — emanated from the Miottis' workshop and bear their trade-mark: they are distinguished by the warm-coloured vitreous material and the very fine decorations. As we have already seen, milk-glass was not an absolute novelty, having also been used in earlier centuries, when it was introduced in the form of threads welded onto the surface of the glass. The 18th century also saw a revival of so-called chalcedony glass used to produce the most varied shapes and blown like ordinary glass to form cups, saucers, tumblers, compote-jars, flower vases and perfume flasks. The 18th century may be called the great originator of coloured vitreous pastes of various types and in a scale of colours and compositions showing a wonderful wealth of variety and ranging from milk-glass to opaline glass in pale blue tones, from deep blue to lapis lazuli blue, to 'malachite' glass and all the various imitations of variegated hard stone, from onyx to one of the most curious original inventions of the Muranese, *avventurina*. This strange name, implying 'accidental', is said to be due to the entirely chance discovery of this extraordinary

PL.

FIG.

PL.

PL.

50

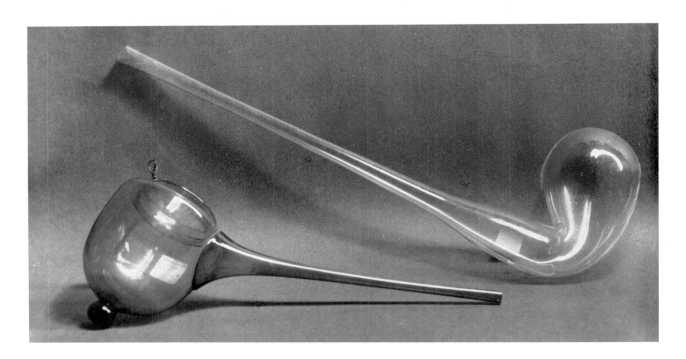

liv VENETIAN PHARMACEUTICAL GLASSES (18TH CENTURY). VENICE, CA' REZZONICO. *lv* VENETIAN RETORTS OR ALEMBICS (18TH CENTURY). VENICE, CA' REZZONICO.

lvi VENETIAN PHARMACEUTICAL VESSEL AND HOUR GLASS (18TH CENTURY). VENICE, SALVIATI-CAMERINO COLLECTION. *lvii* VENETIAN GLASS DISTILLING VESSELS (18TH CENTURY). VENICE, CA' REZZONICO.

Mi porto da Muran, e tazze, e goti
Bozze, impolete, e veri d'ogni sorte
E togo anca in barato i veri roti .

51

paste, or more probably to the difficulty of its manufacture, the secret of which was held by the Miotti family after the beginning of the 17th century. Its unmistakable characteristic was the glitter of copper powder contained in the paste itself: *avventurina* was not only used to give greater variety and interest by the inclusion of tiny parts in other materials —

67 malachite, chalcedony, etc. — but also on its own to produce objects which were generally small and of an ornamental nature: small plates of glass from which, with the aid of a gilded metal framework, very charming caskets and snuff-boxes were constructed, as well as the handles of cutlery and knobs for sticks and umbrellas. Slabs of clear glass, combined with milk-glass, were widely used in the construction of the famous *trionfi*, or table centres. This was a typical 18th century invention, which seems to have been a speciality of Briati and was devised to fill the great empty spaces in the centre of the tables used for the banquets given by the Doges and the nobility, adding a lustre to the whole service of china, silver, ordinary glassware and more precious vessels. These *trionfi*, which were made up of a number of different parts fitted together, generally took the form of tiny works of architecture

76 or of miniature gardens, including green lawns, multicoloured flowers, columns and balustrades, vases and statues, trees and fountains of spun glass.

The craftsmen who constructed these amusing objects were not inferior in patience and imagination to those who, employing the open flames traditionally used for making beads and *conterie*, created tiny mangers, *carillon* figures and artificial flowers to be used as knick-knacks, and indoor shrines. Finally glass, in the form of small plaques, columns and knobs, also found a place in the furniture industry. There are some examples, though not many, of armchairs, candelabra, consoles and so on, in which intagliated and gilded wood is enriched with small pieces of coloured glass, mostly of a pale and almost transparent blue, producing the effect of a lively inlay.

The same technique of glass tessellation was also employed to decorate small corner cupboards, miniature table secrétaires, small safes PL. 79 and cabinets, constructed on the same lines as larger pieces of furniture. In such cases glass was evidently employed as a substitute for the hard stones, marbles and precious inlays in the creation of which Italian, and in particular Florentine, cabinet-makers were so skilled.

Another activity in which Muranese glassmakers displayed true genius and which reached full flowering in the Rococo period, was the art of the mirror. Mirrors now assumed considerable proportions and were an indispensable ornament on drawing-room walls, where they took the place of the hoods above the marble fire-places, and also on the simpler stucco fire-places of boudoirs. In addition, constructed in the most varied measurements and shapes and framed in gilded wood, they were used to reflect and multiply the light of the wall candles, thus giving birth to the bizarre *lumiere*, or combinations of mirrors and candles, which formed part of the total system of illumination employed in the sumptuous 18th century home. As we have already seen, the mirror had been for some time a speciality of Venetian craftsmen and in great demand. In spite of keen French competition — since the time of Colbert — the Venetians held their lead by virtue of the fantastic variety of shapes and the subtle elegance of the decorations they produced. In addition to the mirrors themselves, the frames enclosing them are also made of glass and highly elaborate, being embellished with foliage, arabesques and applied flowers, and with motifs, some of them figurative, engraved with the wheel. To obviate the difficulties of blowing excessively large plates of glass, various smaller slabs were joined together so as to form the most varied patterns, the component parts being attached to one another by metal supports in such a way as to produce a sparkling multiplicity of reflections. The manufacture of an 18th century mirror was a long and complex process. It involved two successive phases and hence was carried out in two different places. In fact, the Murano workshops provided the plates of glass, prepared by a system called *a corona*, that is by blowing cylinders of glass, which were then slit and flattened on a stone; these were then smoothed off and polished and finally completed with a backing of tin amalgam, a process which was carried out in special laboratories situated in Venice. The decorations engraved with the wheel were also executed for preference in Venetian workshops by specialist engravers; this was particularly the case during the second half of the century. The fame, and hence the commercial advantages, enjoyed by Venetian mirrors continued until the fall of the Republic, in spite of the stubborn competition of the French factories. Not until the 19th century were these mirrors replaced by those manufactured by mechanical methods, which were simple and rapid and produced mirrors that were faultless but devoid of all artistic feeling.

Venice also held its lead in another field, in which it was superseded, though not until much later, only by the nascent Bohemian industry: the manufacture of chandeliers.

It has not yet been possible to establish with sufficient accuracy the date of birth of the hanging chandeliers made entirely of glass, an undisputed Muranese speciality. It is a curious fact that contemporary paintings, far into the 18th century, show only the magnificent chandeliers of intagliated wood or gilded metal with many branches each bearing a candle and decorated with a profusion of leaves and flowers. Some interesting specimens of this type, made of copper and undoubtedly of rather late date, are still preserved, for example in Venice in the ballroom of the Ca' Rezzonico. These facts lead us to infer that the invention, or at least the distribution of glass chandeliers took place at a late date, although certain recently published documents speak of a courageous artist, Giuseppe Briati (died in 1772), and his skill in constructing ceiling chandeliers (called

FIG. *xlvii*

ciocche, or 'locks of hair'). It goes without saying that for some time glass parts, in the form of plates, had been applied to the metal skeleton of the lanterns either carried by hand or attached to the façades of Venetian *palazzi* in order to light up landing-stages by the canals at night; the same is true of the monumental single or triple lights on the poops of galleys. But the true glass chandelier was a brilliant product of the mid-18th century. It contained no metal beyond a thin, light, concealed skeleton, indispensable to hold together the various pieces fitted into one another to form the branches and the whole complex structure of its strange architecture. We must not forget that before assuming the simple shape known as columnar, that is to say mounted on a single central rod-like support running down from the ceiling, the hanging lamp followed fanciful patterns sometimes reminiscent of an oriental building (for which reason it was called *a pagoda* and also *alla cinese*), made up of a miraculous aerial tangle of suspended branches further enriched by multicoloured flowers, pendants, curled-up leaves and wreaths of flowers, in short by a whole decorative apparatus breath-taking in its effect. Indeed, the Venetians could not have conceived anything at once so delicate and so extraordinary as these architectural chandeliers, nor anything better suited to the immensely luxurious interiors of the last century of Venice's grandeur, summing up in a single construction the whole magnificence, fanciful delicacy and fragility that characterised the furnishings of the period.

The few examples still to be found intact in certain patrician *palazzi* — for instance the great polychrome chandelier in the Ca' Rezzonico and the no less important one in the Fondazione Querini Stampaglia — give us a clear idea of what they were like and fully explain the great favour and admiration which they aroused in Europe until Bohemia succeeded in imposing its own chandeliers, which were colourless but flashing with a thousand lights from their faceted gems of purest crystal. Briati, a brilliant artist, also succeeded in imitating these chandeliers, after which Muranese glass-works set about producing glass as clear

PL.

as crystal to meet the new competition. Venetian craftsmen began to work with the cutting-wheel, a method explicitly referred to as working *alla boema*, 'in the Bohemian manner,' copying shapes and patterns in the big, heavy ceremonial beakers decorated with coats of arms, medallions, or emblems of the Doges, and cutting bottles and carafes, candlesticks, plates and dishes, fruit stands and in general all the articles intended for use on the tables of the nobility. It must be said, however, that their material certainly did not display the qualities of hardness and transparency possessed by the models from beyond the Alps; moreover the Venetian craftsman rarely succeeded in manifesting signs of a sincere inspiration as embodied in some happy invention, or in asserting himself as against the foreign competitor by the fineness of his own cutting technique. He was perhaps more at ease in glasses where colour regained its supremacy: in the graceful milk-glass which continued to be produced in every possible shape, in glass pastes and in the *conterie* used to make artificial jewellery and decorative motifs for the most varied purposes; and finally in pictorial decoration, in which artists of great taste and ability assisted the work of the glass-maker. Thus the link with painting and the art of the print and the miniature, which had been operative and fertile during the Italian Renaissance, was restored. It will be enough to refer as an example to those curious transcriptions in black or sepia of engravings by Canaletto, Brustolon, Visentini and others, on plates of white milk-glass — intended to be framed and hung up as pictures — showing views of Venice, feasts of the Doges and similar subjects. We must also recall the very numerous glass pictures painted with great technical skill on the back of the glass, reproducing well known subjects by other artists, from Tiepolo to Guardi, Pietro Longhi, Piazzetta, Magiotto, and so on, generally copied indirectly from prints — undoubtedly a lively and popular means of propagating the works of the greatest artists of the day. From here

it was only a short step to the painting of humbler objects such as ordinary table-ware. In fact, especially during the second half of the century, we may observe such activities being carried on with great success by a family of artists, the Brussas. They specialised in the enamel decoration of beakers, carafes, bottles and table-ware in general, made of common transparent glass, which they embellished with flowers, birds, animals, fruit and also sacred and profane figure compositions, as may be seen in the copious material available in the Murano museum. It is perhaps unnecessary to add that these products too tended to make up by quantity for what they lacked in quality, since their colours were sometimes dull and inferior and the designs for the most part reminiscent of folk art. The Brussas and their colleagues evidently pandered to the taste of the mass of the uncultured public, while the pieces worked *alla boema*, whole sets of which were ground and cut into facets and edged with gold, were reserved for the tables of the nobility. But as the century proceeds we shall search in vain, in a production that was often too rapid and abundant to be of high quality, for signs of any new idea of the re-emergence of a purer tradition. It seems that to offset these deficiences of quality, glass-makers strove after strangeness and eccentricity: they made trumpets and other musical instruments of glass, curious bottles in the shape of pistols and guns, vases and receptacles shaped like boots, as well as complete sets of all-glass cutlery, hanging containers for holy water and other amusing small objects. The manufacture of glassware for medical, pharmaceutical and other technical purposes once more became abundant in 18th-century Venice. We may form a concrete idea of these products by visiting the reconstruction of an 18th century pharmacy under the sign of the 'Due San Marchi' in the Ca' Rezzonico, complete with back-shop and laboratory, with chemist's furnaces, retorts, alembics, serpentines and other curious instruments undoubtedly manufactured at Murano. We shall also find

lvi

PLS. 70-72

FIGS. xlviii, l

FIGS. xlix, liii, lvii

PL. 73

FIG. li

57

smaller objects and vases which are perfect in proportion and elegance of line, although devoid of special decorations, and which are in the noblest tradition of artistic glassware. On the other hand we can observe in the commoner and more heterogeneous field of what might be called commercial production, obvious signs of flagging inspiration and technical negligence. The repertory is as vast as it is often poor in quality: pierced-work baskets, glass fruit imitating the real thing in shape and colour, and articles for various purposes in which there is a return to old techniques, ranging from white or coloured net-glass to milk-glass and glass blown in a single colour, sometimes very dark, and then decorated with gold. Milk-glass was used to model statuettes and small groups, Moors, birds and animals, as though in competition with porcelain. The 18th century also saw a revival of the apparently obsolete *conterie* industry. These many and varied objects were sold in Venice itself by the Muranese masters and, after the abolition of the traditional *stazioneri*, in special shops situated — as we are informed by the *Mariegola dell'Arte* — under the Procuratie Nuove. The Fiera della Sensa, held on Ascension Day in St. Mark's Square, which inspired among others a vivid painting by Francesco Guardi, was always a magnificent occasion that attracted large crowds, while the vast number of master glass-makers and workshops seemed to suggest that Murano was heading for its heyday.

The reality was soon to prove quite different. Events followed one another in rapid succession in the political sphere, and upon them depended the fate of the crafts and industries bound up with commerce and the economic life of the State. The last decades of the 18th century, characterised by those aspirations and manifestations in the field of glass-making which we have already described, saw the rise of other centres in countries that no longer imported anything from Murano, having now their own illustrious glass-making tradition, such as Belgium and Holland, and even England, whose flint glass was to offer serious competition to the Bohemians themselves, and also Germany, particularly through its Bohemian factories. The diminished capacity for expansion, already perceptible at the beginning of the century, returned after the happy revival due to the stimulus afforded by Briati. This diminished capacity for expansion, now linked with excessive technical carelessness, accelerated the crisis already manifest before the dramatic events of 1797. The fall of the Republic naturally delivered the *coup de grâce*, bringing about a cessation of all activity and drying up the living springs of commerce and export.

Thus Murano entered the 19th century in a state of absolute decline which even included the disbanding of the Guild of Glass-Makers. All that survived, apart from a limited manufacture of utilitarian articles, were a few workshops producing beads *a lume*; the majority of the workshops on the island closed their shutters. Not until a few decades later, with the courageous efforts of a few Muranese still mindful of the ancient glories, was an attempt made to find the lost road and reconquer the technical procedures. There then followed a long period of preparation and study accompanied by rare flashes of lively originality. This, therefore, seems the right point at which to terminate our discussion. Simply to complete the picture we shall mention that the crisis, though profound — a crisis of inspiration rather than of technical skill — was averted and became the occasion for a reawakening brought about by those few who were impelled to attempt a revival in the face of every possible difficulty. Through them, at a time when all the other centres in Italy, including Altare, had ceased all activity, Murano alone achieved in silence and labour the necessary prerequisites for the modern revival.

Above all we must note the importance to this rebirth of the founding shortly after the middle of the last century, on the initiative of the Abbot Vincenzo Zanetti, of a museum on the island itself: here, along with ancient relics, there were also collected the best products which gradually emerged from the new artistic forces now at work. In conjunction with the museum, a school of design was set up that proved of the utmost value in leading the younger generation to a study of forms and the resumption of traditional techniques. Thus the two institutions, which were closely connected, were not long in bearing fruit, while ardent scholars — from Zanetti himself to Cecchetti and Santi — continued their researches in the historical field, thereby increasing awareness of the glorious past. Today the old museum, now amalgamated with the Teodoro Correr collections of Venetian glass, has given birth to what is perhaps the richest, and certainly the most singular, collection of glass — from archaelogical epochs down to modern times — anywhere in Europe.

This 'excursus' was intended to be an outline, as informed as possible though brief, of the general course of events which are sometimes so complex and hard to disentangle. Moments of total obscurity — the High Middle Ages in the Roman province, for example — alternate with periods extremely well attested by documentary and material evidence. The bibliography, which we have considered it useful to append, will disclose to the reader the disparity and discontinuity of the studies that have been undertaken. It will be noted that, while there is a comparative shortage of literature dealing with the finds and technical details of ancient glass — that of Rome in particular — the Muranese industry is more widely dealt with in treatises of recent date. On the other hand, exhaustive studies of the particular activities of other Italian centres, beginning with that

lix DECORATIVE JUG AND VASE. MURANESE ART (LATE 19TH CENTURY). FORMERLY FORTUNY COLLECTION, NOW AT MURANO, MUSEO VETRARIO.

59

of Altare, are few or altogether lacking. Tuscany alone has been the subject of a very recent monograph that has finally opened up the path to this field of exploration, which we should like to see systematised and extended to the minor centres too. We may perhaps hope that the present work, though necessarily generalised in character, may give others in a better position to do so, the wish to collect documentary and material evidence, the study of which will gradually enlarge the view we have of the whole of Italy. This would help to clarify the various problems connected with the technology of glass-blowing and with the commercial and cultural exchanges within the ambit of our civilisation at all periods. Such studies should include not only the major works of genius but also the more modest contributions, which are of no less vital importance because they are closer to the common understanding and to ordinary, everyday taste. The resulting knowledge will be another step towards the better understanding of those industrial arts which, especially in Italy, passed, in thousands of different branches, through moments of splendid brilliance.

BIBLIOGRAPHY

a) *GENERAL: TECHNOLOGY, SOURCES, HISTORY OF EUROPEAN GLASS, CATALOGUES.*

TEOFILO: *Schedula diversarum artium* (mid 10th century).

VASARI, G.: *Le Vite* . . . (Introduction), Florence 1550.

AGRICOLA [G. BAUER]: *De re metallica*, Basle 1556.

NERI, A.: *L'arte vetraria*, Florence 1612 (subsequent editions: Venice 1663; Milan 1818; London 1662; Amsterdam 1668; Amsterdam-Danzig 1679; Paris 1752).

LABARTE, J.: *Les arts industriels*, Paris 1875.

GERSPACH, E.: *L'art de la verrerie*, Paris 1885.

VOPEL, H.: *Die altchristl. Goldgläser*, Fribourg 1889.

FIGUIER, G.: *Les merveilles de l'industrie*, Paris n. d.

VIGREUX, H.: *Le soufflage du verre*, Paris 1920.

BUCKLEY, W.: *European Glass*, London 1926.

HONEY, W. B.: *Glass. Guide to the Museum Coll.*, Victoria and Albert Museum, London 1946.

SIDNEY LEWIS, J.: *Old Glass and how to collect it*, London 1948.

CINI, M. - FRANCESCHINI, F. - ROMAGNOLI, G.: *Lezioni di tecnica vetraria*, Venice 1949.

BARRELET, J.: *La verrerie en France*, Paris 1953.

MARIACHER, G.: *L'arte del vetro*, Milan 1954.

VAVRA, J. R.: *Das Glas*. Prague 1954.

CHAMBON, R.: *Histoire de la verrerie en Belgique*, Brussels, 1955.

Glass from the Corning Museum, Corning New York 1955.

Trois millénaires d'art verrier, Musée Curtius, Liege 1958.

'Journal of Glass Studies,' I, Corning Glass Center, New York 1959.

b) *ANTIQUITY: FROM EGYPT TO ROME.*

PLINY: *Naturalis Historia* (1st century A. D.), modern edition, Rome 1946.

KISA, A.: *Das Glas im Altertume*, Leipzig 1908.

SANGIORGI, G.: *Collezione di vetri antichi*, Milan - Rome 1914.

BRUSIN, G., *Aquileja*, Udine 1929.

HARDEN, D. B.: *Roman Glass from Karamis*, in 'University of Michigan Studies,' XLI, Ann Arbor 1936.

NEUBURG, F.: *Glass in Antiquity*, London 1949.

ZECCHIN, L.: *Vetro di Plinio*, in 'Giornale Economico' (Venice), January-February 1951.

HARDEN, D. B.: *Vasa Murrina*, in 'Journal of Roman Studies,' XXXIX (1949) and XLIV (1954).

CECCHELLI, C.: *La vita di Roma nel Medio Evo*, I. *Arti Minori* (3), Rome n. d. (and *Supplem.*, Rome 1960).

RIEGL, A.: *Spätrömische Kunstindustrie*, Italian edition, Florence 1953.

ZECCHINI, L.: *Vetri al Museo di Adria*, in 'Giornale Economico' (Venice), 1956.

Glass from the Ancient World, The Ray Winfield Smith Collection, Corning Glass Center, New York 1957.

CLASINA ISINGS: *Roman Glass from dated Finds*, Groeningen 1957.

Iridescenze e colori di vetri antichi. Catalogue edited by R. PINCELLI, C. VOLPE, R. GUALANDI, with preface by L. LAURENZI, Bologna 1959.

MOREY, C. R.: *The gold-glass Coll. of the Vatican Library*, Vatican City 1959.

c) *VENICE.*

Capitolare dell'Arte Vetraria, 1271 (published by G. MONTICOLO, *I Capitolari delle arti veneziane*, II, Rome 1905).

Mariegola dei verieri (vetrai), 1441, Original edition in the Museo Civico Correr at Venice; two others, dated 1525 and 1618, in the Museo Vetrario at Murano.

MARTINO DA CANALE: *Cronaca* (CCLXXXI - July 1268), modern edition, Florence 1845.

FILARETE [AVERULINO, A.]: *Trattato di Architettura* (c. 1450-1475), German edition, Vienna 1890.

ARETINO, P.: *Lettere* (1531), modern edition, Milan 1957, Vols. I and II.

BIRINGUCCIO, V.: *De la pirotecnia*, Venice 1540.

ALBERTI, L.: *Descrittione di tutta Italia*, Venice 1551.

SABELLICO, M. A.: *De Venetae urbis situ*, Basle 1560.

FIORAVANTI, L.: *Dello specchio di scientia universale*, Venice 1572.

GARZONI, T.: *La piazza universale*, etc., Venice 1585.

GOZZI, G.: *Del vetro*, Venice 1794 (discussed by L. Zecchini in 'Giornale Economico,' 1951).

MOSCHINI, G. A.: *Guida per l'isola di Murano*, Venice 1808.

NEIJMAN RIZZI, C.: *L'Isola di Murano*, Venice 1811 (ms. in the Museo Civico Correr).

SAGREDO, A.: *Sulle consorterie delle arti edificative*, etc., Venice 1856.

CECCHETTI, B.: *Sulla storia dell'arte vetraria muranese*, Venice 1865.

ZANETTI, V.: *Guida di Murano*, Venice 1866.

CECCHETTI, B.: *Della filatura e tessitura del vetro*, Venice 1867.

CECCHETTI, B. - ZANETTI, V. - SANFERMO, E.: *Monografia della vetraria veneziana e muranese*, Venice 1874.

ZANETTI, V.: *Degli specchi di Venezia*, Venice 1877.

— *Il libro d'oro di Murano*, Venice 1883.

URBANI DE GHELTOF, G. M.: *Les arts industriels à Venise*, Venice 1885.

61

SANTI, A.: *Origine dell'arte vetraria in Venezia e Murano*, Venice 1886.

MOLINIER, E.: *Venise, ses arts décoratifs*, etc., Paris 1889.

LEVI, C. A.: *L'arte del vetro in Murano nel Rinascimento*, Venice 1895.

SCHMIDT, R.: *Die venezianischen Emailgläser*, etc., in 'Jahrb. d. königl. preuss. Kunstsamml.,' XXXII, 1911.

LORENZETTI, G.: *Una fiaschetta di lattimo*, in 'Dedalo,' 1920, I.

MORAZZONI, G.: *Il lattimo veneziano*, ibid., 1923-24.

LORENZETTI, G.: *Venezia e il suo estuario*, Milan-Rome 1926; 2nd edition, Rome 1956.

MOLMENTI, P.: *La storia di Venezia nella vita privata*, Bergamo 1928.

MORAZZONI, G.: *L'arte del vetro a Venezia nel Settecento: lo specchio*, in 'Dedalo,' 1929-30.

LORENZETTI, G.: *Vetri di Murano*, Rome 1931.

— *Murano e l'arte del vetro soffiato*, in 'Emporium,' 1936.

BETTINI, S.: *La pittura Bizantina: i mosaici*, Florence 1939.
— *Mosaici antichi di San Marco*, Bergamo 1944.

ZECCHIN, L.: *Colbert e gli specchi veneziani*, in 'Giornale Economico' (Venice), 1950.

SCHLOSSER, J.: *Venezianische Gläser*, Vienna 1951 (Catalogue of the Museum).

ZECCHIN, L.: *L'Archivio annesso al Museo Vetrario di Murano*, in 'Giornale Economico' (Venice), 1951.
— *Sulla storia dell'arte vetraria muranese*, ibid., 1952.

GALLO, R.: *Contributi alla storia dell'arte del vetro di Murano*, in 'Giornale Economico' (Venice), 1953.

— *Giuseppe Briati e l'arte del vetro a Murano nel secolo XVIII*, Venice 1953.

GASPARETTO, A.: *Decorazione a smalto su vetro islamica e veneziana*, in 'Giornale Economico' (Venice), 1953.

— *Nuove ipotesi sulle origini della vetraria veneziana*, in 'Ateneo Veneto,' 1953.

LORENZETTI, G.: *Guida del Museo Vetrario di Murano*, Venice 1953.

MORAZZONI, G.: *Le conterie veneziane*, Venice 1953.

MARIACHER, G.: *I vetri della raccolta Maglione presso il Museo Vetrario di Murano*, in 'Giornale Economico' (Venice), 1954.

ZECCHIN, L.: *Sulla storia delle conterie veneziane*, ibid., October 1953 (*Un curioso manoscritto*); November 1953 (*Storia delle storie*); January 1954 (*L'avventurina*); April 1954 (*Contarie e conterie*); June 1954 (*L'espatrio dell'arte*).

ZUFFA, M.: *I vetri del Museo Civico di Bologna*, in 'La Mercanzia' (Bologna), 1954.

GASPARETTO, A.: *Sviluppo delle forme nella vetraria muranese*, in 'Vetro e silicati,' 3, 1936.

ZECCHIN, L.: *Antichi disegni di vetri muranesi*, in 'Giornale Economico,' April 1957.

MARIACHER, G.: *Antichi lampadari vitrei veneziani*, Venice 1957.

— *I 'lattimi' dei Miotti al Museo Vetrario di Murano*, in 'Boll. dei Musei Civici Veneziani,' 2, 1958.

Three great Centuries of Venetian Glass, Corning Glass Center, New York 1958.

GASPARETTO, A.: *Il vetro di Murano dalle origini ad oggi*, Venice 1958.

MARIACHER, G.: *I vetri della raccolta Fortuny*, in 'Giornale Economico' (Venice), 1959.
— *Vetri inediti in raccolte private*, ibid., 1959.

ZECCHIN, L.: *Note di storia dell'arte vetraria muranese*, ibid., 1959.
— *Un vetraio del '500: Nicolò Dell'Aquila*, ibid., 1959.

d) OTHER ITALIAN AND FOREIGN CENTRES; THE SPREAD OF THE 'FAÇON DE VENISE'.

HOUDOY, J. M.: *Verreries à la façon de Venise. La fabrication flamande*, etc., Paris 1873.

PINCHART, A.: *Les fabriques de verres de Venise, d'Anvers et de Bruxelles au XVIe et XVIIe siècle*, in 'Bull. des Commissions Royales d'Art et d'Archéologie,' 1882-1883.

VAN DE CASTEELE, E.: *Ancienne fabrication de verres de Venise à Namur*, in 'Annales de la Société Archéologique de Namur,' 1884.

SCHUERMANS, H.: *Verre liégeois 'façon de Venise' etc., au XVIIe siècle*, in 'B. I. A. L.,' 1885.

— *Verre à la façon de Venise et d'Altare fabriqué à Châtelet au XVIIe siècle*, in 'Documents et Rapports de la Société Archéol. de Charleroi,' 1886.

— *Verre façon de Venise aux Pays-Bas*, in 'Bull. des Commissions Royales d'Art et d'Archéol.,' 1883-93.

NOVI, G.: *Dell'arte vetraria nelle province meridionali*, Naples 1888-89.

VAN DE CASTEELE, E.: *Verreries de Venise à Gand*, in 'Messager des Sciences historiques,' 1891.

FAVARO, A.: *Intorno ai cannocchiali costruiti e usati da Galileo Galilei*, Venice 1901.

CISCATO, A.: *Arte vetraria in Padova*, Padua 1902.

BOULMONT, A.: *La verrerie, etc., dans les Ardennes*, Dôle 1906.

AVENA, A.: *L'Arte vetraria in Verona*, in 'Madonna Verona,' 1911.

FROTINGHAM, A. W.: *Hispanic Glass*, New York 1941.

HONEY, W. B.: *English Glass*, London 1946.

ZECCHIN, L.: *Bernardo Perrotto vetraio altarese*, in 'Giornale Economico,' December 1949 - February 1950.

— *Vetrerie dell'Accademia del Cimento* ('Quaderni del Liceo di Storia della Scienza'), Florence 1950.

TADDEI, G.: *L'arte del vetro in Firenze*, Florence 1954.

CHAMBON, R., *Histoire de la verrerie en Belgique*, Brussels 1955.

FROTINGHAM, A. W.: *Barcelona Glass in Venetian Style*, New York, Hispanic Society, 1956.

GASPARETTO, A.: *Nuovi studi sulla vetraria 'façon de Venise' nei Paesi Bassi*, in 'Arte Veneta,' 1956.

ZECCHIN, L.: *I cannocchiali di Galilei e gli occhialeri veneziani*, in 'Giornale Economico' (Venice), 1957.
— *Antiche vetrerie veronesi*, ibid., July 1957.

I saggi di naturali esperienze fatti nell'Accademia del Cimento, Florence 1667; *Strumenti e suppellettili della medesima Accademia conservati presso il Museo di Storia della Scienza di Firenze* (edition edited by the 'Domus Galileana' and the Museum itself, with catalogues and notes by M. L. BONELLI), Pisa 1957.

BONELLI, M. L.: *Gli strumenti superstiti dell'Accademia del Cimento*, Pisa 1958.

MARIACHER, G.: *La raccolta dei vetri spagnoli al Museo Vetrario di Murano*, in 'Giornale Economico,' 1958.

PLATES

Plate 1

Two-handled amphora of ovoid shape without foot; produced by pouring into a mould and
subsequently polishing with the grindstone (from Felsinian tombs dating from the 6th cent. B.C.)
Phoenician art (6th cent. B.C.)

Bologna, Museo Civico

Plate 2

Small jug of 'oinochoe' type and small amphora of vitreous paste, the former with round flat foot,
the latter with a small discoid foot, with poured polychrome decoration (from an Etruscan tomb)
Etruscan art (?) (5th cent. B.C.)

Bologna, Museo Civico

Plate 3

Small 'oinochoe' type amphora with handle of green glass applied to a body of coloured pastes;
technique combining moulding and pouring
Egyptian or Mediterranean art (*c*. 2nd cent. B.C.)

Solid block of iridescent glass
Roman art (?) (1st cent. A.D.)

Murano, Museo Vetrario

Plate 4

Two small plates of 'millefiori' type and small footless bowl with painted decorations
Alexandrian art (1st cent. A.D.)

Turin, Museo Greco-Romano

Plate 5

Cinerary urn with flat lid, of green glass
Roman art (1st-2nd cent. A.D.)

Murano, Museo Vetrario

Plate 6
Small balm flask in the shape of a bird, and spherical cinerary urn with bell-shaped lid
Roman art (1st-2nd cent. A.D.)
Bologna, Museo Civico

Plate 7
Beaker in the shape of a truncated cone with an embossed pattern blown in a metal mould.
Flask and bottle of translucent glass
Roman art (1st-2nd cent. A.D.)

Bologna, Museo Civico

Murano, Museo Vetrario

Plate 9
Small footed bowl with two handles and bulbous bottle with long neck decorated with applied horizontal threads
Roman art (1st-2nd cent. A.D.)

Murano, Museo Vetrario

Plate 10

Bottle with long neck and bottle of square section, of blown glass. Small two-handled bowl
with low foot, pressed and finished with the grindstone, after the 'pterotoi' type
Roman art (1st–2nd cent. A.D.)

Bologna, Museo Civico

Plate 11

Blown glass bottle with handle, speckled with white. Small gadrooned bowl blown on mould
Roman art (1st-2nd cent. A.D.)

Bologna, Museo Civico

Plate 12
Bottles of various shapes and sizes of transparent blown glass
Roman art (1st-2nd cent. A.D.)
Murano, Museo Vetrario

Plate 13
Footless cup with handle of greenish-blue glass
Roman art (1st-2nd cent. A.D.)
Murano, Museo Vetrario

Plate 14

Bottle of square section of transparent glass. Small bottle of opaque glass with handle
Roman art (1st-2nd cent. A.D.)

Small bottle with square base, and bearing a seal (the figure of Mercury)
Syrian art (3rd cent. A.D.)

Turin, Museo Greco-Romano

Plate 15

Bulbous cinerary urn of coloured glass
Roman art (1st-2nd cent. A.D.)

Bologna, Museo Civico

Plate 16
Spherical urn with conical lid and rounded foot, moulded and finished with the grindstone.
Small footless bowl worked in the same way
Roman art (1st-2nd cent. A.D.)

Turin, Museo Greco-Romano

Plate 17
Double balm flask with threads applied in a continuous spiral
Syrian art (4th cent. A.D.)

Small animal in blown glass and small vase with footless spherical body and handle
Roman art (3rd–4th cent. A.D.)

Murano, Museo Vetrario

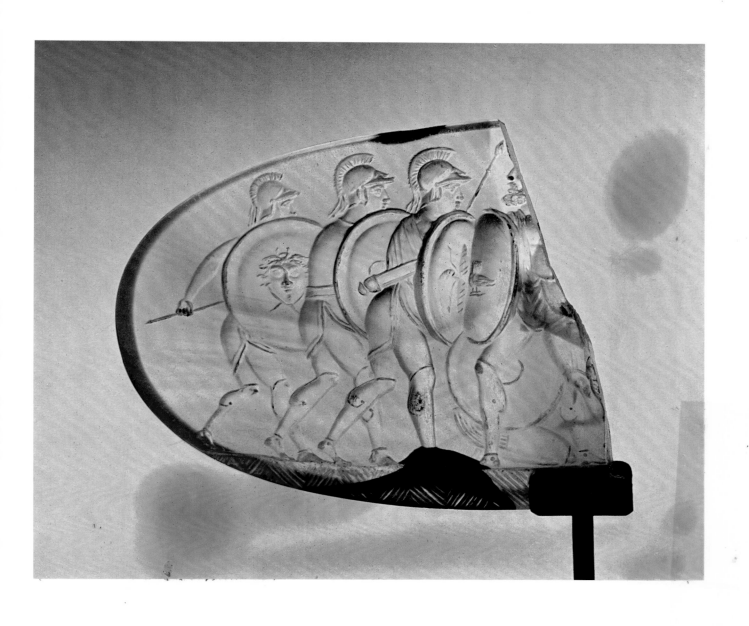

Plate 18

Fragment of a plaque engraved with a battle scene; thick glass cut with the wheel
Hellenistic art (3rd cent. A.D.)

Murano, Museo Vetrario

Plate 19

Fragment of a bowl of translucent glass, bearing a hunting scene engraved with the grindstone
Alexandrian art (*c.* 3rd-4th cent. A.D.)

Murano, Museo Vetrario

Plate 20

Jug of thick glass; exhumed in Murano (1878), perhaps a rare specimen of local production
(*c.* 14th cent.)

Murano, Museo Vetrario

Plate 21

Nuptial goblet attributed to the Baroviers, decorated with portraits of the bride and bridegroom
and allegorical scenes in multicoloured and gold enamels: we see here the 'Fountain of Love'
Venetian art (*c.* 1460-70)

Murano, Museo Vetrario

Plate 22

Liturgical chalice with a high foot, the lower part of the bowl decorated with prominent ribs in imitation of metal types; enamel decoration representing the 'Flight into Egypt', the 'Adoration of the Magi' and two medallions with busts of prophets
Venetian art (*c.* 1460)

Bologna, Museo Civico

Plate 23

Nuptial goblet painted in enamel with medallions of the bride and bridegroom inside laurel wreaths, and cupids
Venetian art (c. 1480)

London, British Museum

Plate 24

Goblet with a high foot and cylindrical body; enamel decoration depicting the 'Triumph of Justice'
Venetian art (*c.* 1480)

Florence, Museo Nazionale

Plate 25
Nuptial goblet with a low foot, painted with polychrome and gold enamels depicting
the ' Procession of Venus ' (?) in a landscape
Venetian art (c. 1480)

London, British Museum

Plate 26
Hanging mosque lamp in the shape of a bell; enamel decorations showing geometrical motifs and Arabic inscriptions
Syrian art (15th cent.)

Florence, Museo Nazionale

Plate 27
Jug and small pail of transparent glass decorated in polychrome enamels with plant patterns
Venetian art (late 15th cent.)

Murano, Museo Vetrario

Plate 28

Ribbed chalice with high base in the shape of a bell; small enamel decorations
Venetian art (late 15th cent.)

Bologna, Museo Civico

Plate 29

Beaker with moulded ribs decorated with enamel dots and scales round the rim; traces of gilding
Venetian art (late 15th cent.)

Turin, Museo Civico

Plate 30

Goblet in the shape of a pyx inspired by Gothic metal types, with ribs and lid;
decorated with gilt and a small pattern in coloured enamels
Venetian art (late 15th cent.)

London, Victoria and Albert Museum

Plate 31

Large chalice with conical bowl and foot (the knot has been restored with a metal frame);
enamel decorations showing the arms of the Sforzas
Venetian art (c. 1470-80)

Milan, Museo del Castello Sforzesco

Plate 32

Small hemispherical bowl with a smooth surface decorated with a small pattern in enamel and containing a bust of St Anthony of Padua
Venetian art (*c.* 1470-80)

Milan, Museo Poldi Pezzoli

Plate 34

Drinking-glass with foot sprayed with gold. The bowl is transparent and painted with
a floral pattern typical of the period (lilies of the valley) in multicoloured enamel
Venetian art (late 15th-early 16th cent.)

London, Victoria and Albert Museum

Plate 35
Covered pyx in milk-glass decorated with blue drops and enamel gilt interlace in relief
Venetian art (late 15th–early 16th cent.)
London, Victoria and Albert Museum

Plate 36

Small jug decorated with enamel dots and two medallions of heraldic type
Venetian art (late 15th cent.)

London, Victoria and Albert Museum

Plate 37
Large bowl with round foot and stem blown into a mould; decorations in a pattern of small scales of polychrome enamel
Venetian art (early 16th cent)

Turin, Museo Civico

Plate 38
Ampulla with handle and high foot of 'chalcedony' glass reminiscent of metal shapes
Venetian art (late 15th cent.)

London, Victoria and Albert Museum

Plate 39

Bottle of 'chalcedony' glass with long neck
Venetian art (early 16th cent.)

London, Victoria and Albert Museum

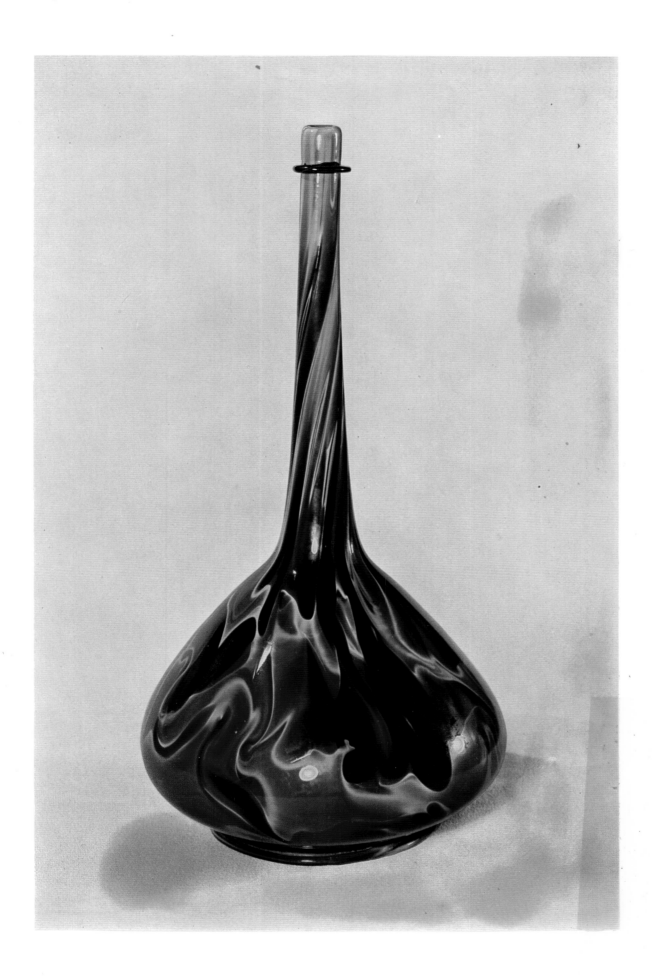

Plate 40
Bowl of 'chalcedony' glass with low foot
Venetian art (early 16th cent.)

Turin, Museo Civico

Plate 41

Jug with handle and spout; the decoration on the dark background consists of small threads
of milk-glass applied round the neck and white enamel on top of the moulded cord pattern on the body of the jug
Venetian art (16th cent.)

Turin, Museo Civico

Plate 42

Goblet with stem, of transparent glass with threads of milk-glass and blue stripes incorporated
Venetian art (early 16th cent.)

Murano, Museo Vetrario

Plate 43

Compote-jar with two handles and a moulded lid, transparent glass decorated with canes and twisted threads
Venetian art (late 16th cent.)

Milan, Museo Poldi Pezzoli

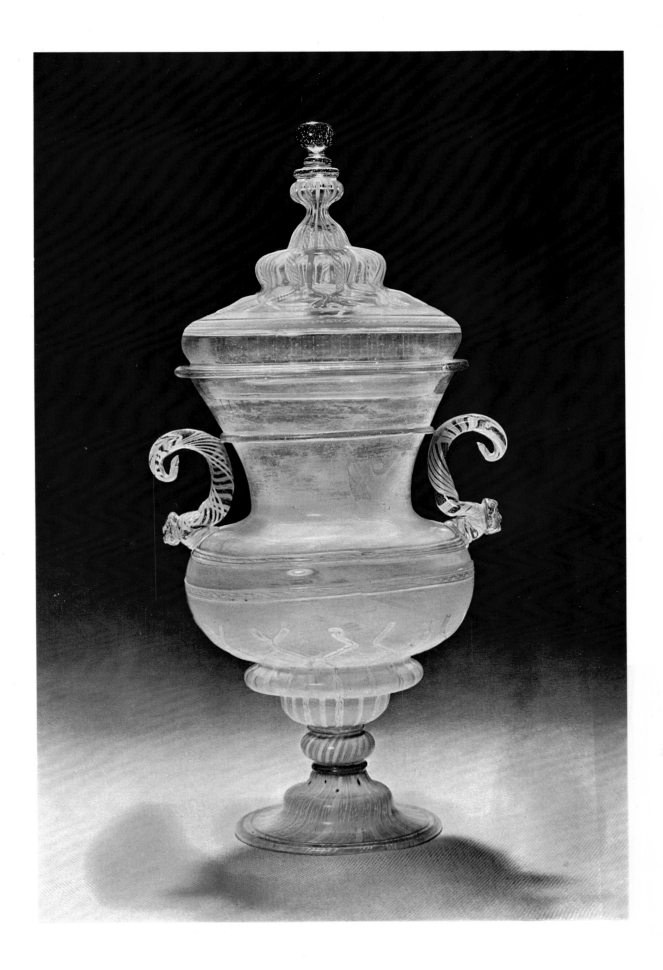

Plate 44
Reliquary on transparent glass with incorporated canes of white net-glass
Venetian art (early 16th cent.)
Murano, Museo Vetrario

Plate 45
Two-handled casket with lid of white net-glass
Venetian art (*c.* mid-16th cent.)

Murano, Museo Vetrario

Plate 46

Small table-stand of smooth glass with incorporated white threads imitating feathers.
Small bottle of hexagonal section decorated with threads of milk-glass applied to the exterior
Venetian art (16th cent.)

Murano, Museo Vetrario

Plate 47
Large gadrooned bowl of net-glass with white threads on alternating canes. In the centre,
'a freddo' painting on the under side, showing a portrait of a lady in profile
Venetian art (*c.* mid-16th cent.)

Turin, Museo Civico

Plate 48
Perfume bottle in the shape of a top with incorporated spiral white threads
Venetian art (late 16th–early 17th cent.)

Murano, Museo Vetrario

Plate 49

Bowl with foot decorated with spiral and net-pattern white and coloured threads in alternating stripes
Venetian art (late 16th-early 17th cent.)

Murano, Museo Vetrario

Plate 50

Water-jug in the shape of a small galley with coloured stamped masks and decorations; attributed to Armenia Vivarini
Venetian art (mid-16th cent.)

Murano, Museo Vetrario

Plate 51
Oil lamp in the shape of a horse; transparent glass with applied ultramarine glass
Venetian art (early 16th cent.)

Murano, Museo Vetrario

Plate 52

Portable flask of flattened shape; decorations scratched with diamond point on monochrome glass
Venetian art (16th cent.)

Turin, Museo Civico

Plate 53
Small ampulla with applied masks and crested handle
Venetian art (mid-16th cent.)

Vase with three spouts and smooth circular foot, decorated with the diamond point
Hall art (?) (Tyrol, late 16th cent.)

Murano, Museo Vetrario

Plate 54

Bowl with very long turned stem, the lower part moulded with masks;
painted and gilded decorations on the stem and the underside of the bowl
Venetian art (late 16th cent.)

Turin, Museo Civico

Plate 55

Chalices of various shapes with stems decorated with wings and open work; transparent glass coloured in some parts, worked with pincers
Venetian art (late 16th-early 17th cent.)

Murano, Museo Vetrario

Plate 56

Small vase with long neck and spherical body
Venetian art inspired by the Orient (late 17th cent.)

Small ampulla crested handle, and dropping-glass (?) in the shape of a bunch of grapes, blown into a mould
Venetian art (16th-17th cent.)

Plate 57
Small ampulla with decorated handle and masks. Jug with handle and lid, decorated with applied polychrome flowerets
Venetian art (late 17th cent.)

Murano, Museo Vetrario

Plate 58

Sheet of glass painted on the back with the 'Supper in Simon's House'
Venetian art (*c.* mid-16th cent.)

Murano, Museo Vetrario

Plate 59

Large plate decorated 'a freddo' on the underside in gilt and colours showing
the 'Judgement of Paris' after a print by M. A. Raimondi
Venetian art (late 16th cent.)

Turin, Museo Civico

Plate 60

Portable mirror with frame and clasp of white metal; glass bearing gilded decorations
Venetian art (late 17th cent.)

Murano, Museo Vetrario

Plate 62

Small amphora of white milk-glass with enamel decorations
Workshop of the Miottis (*c.* mid-18th cent.)

Murano, Museo Vetrario

Plate 63

Small milk-glass snuff-bottle painted with enamels showing the figure of a drinker and (on the reverse side) an old man taking snuff; in addition, writing, flourishes, the date 1767 and the initials of Daniele Miotti
Workshop of Daniele Miotti (1767)

Murano, Museo Vetrario

Plate 64

Small milk-glass plate with polychrome enamel decorations showing flowers and a parrot;
bearing the trade mark 'Al Gesù, Murano' of the Miotti factory (18th cent.)

London, Victoria and Albert Museum

Plate 65

Bottles with long necks and small cylindrical jar with lid, of undecorated milk-glass
Murano, workshop of Bertolinis (?) (18th cent.)

Murano, Museo Vetrario

Plate 67
Two-handled gadrooned bowl of 'chalcedony' glass with patches of 'avventurina' incorporated
Muranese factory (18th cent.)

Murano, Museo Vetrario

Plate 68

Group of various objects of vitreous paste: small 'chalcedony' glass; square perfume bottle of blue glass with patches of 'avventurina';
snuff-box of 'avventurina' and others of white and coloured pastes, with frames of gilded metal
Muranese factories (18th cent.)

Murano, Museo Vetrario

Plate 69

Large ceiling chandelier of white glass with flowers and other polychrome decorations, 'pagoda' shape
Workshop of Briati (?) (*c.* mid-18th cent.)

Venice, Ca' Rezzonico

Plate 70
Beaker painted in enamel with birds and branches
Art of the Brussas (late 18th cent.)

Murano, Museo Vetrario

Plate 71

Cylindrical tumbler with gilded edge and enamel decorations depicting Adam and Eve
Art of the Brussas (late 18th cent.)

Murano, Museo Vetrario

Plate 72
Small liqueur bottles of transparent glass decorated with figures in polychrome enamels
Brussas' workshop (?) (18th cent.)
Venice, Salviati-Camerino Collection

Plate 73
Small barrel decorated with applied threads and two small bottles in the shape of pistols
Venetian art (18th cent.)

Murano, Museo Vetrario

Plate 74

Small basket with open-work handle and rich applied decorations
Venetian art (late 18th cent.)

Murano, Museo Vetrario

Plate 75
Small open-work basket of transparent glass
Venetian art (late 18th cent.)
Murano, Museo Vetrario

Plate 76

Table-centre in the shape of a miniature garden with balustrades, milk-glass urns
and a fountain in the middle; all made of blown and drawn glass and coloured pastes
Venetian art (18th cent.)

Murano, Museo Vetrario

Plate 77
Small round basket and cup and saucer of white and red filigree glass
Venetian art (late 18th cent.)

Murano, Museo Vetrario

Plate 78

Small basket of smooth green glass with applied polychrome decorations of flowers and flourishes;
the fruit is also of polychrome glass
Venetian art (late 18th cent.)

Murano, Museo Vetrario

Plate 79
Small piece of furniture with drawers, modelled on architecture, of wood with polychrome inlays of vitreous paste
Venetian art (late 18th cent.)

Murano, Museo Vetrario

Plate 82

Oil-cruet and two sugar bowls of smooth blue glass, the lid surmounted by a fruit
Venetian art (late 18th cent.)

Murano, Museo Vetrario

Plate 83

Transparent glass bottle containing coloured fruit; decorated with wavy bands applied to the exterior
Venetian art (late 18th-early 19th cent.)

Venice, Salviati-Camerino Collection

Plate 84

Vase with three spouts and a smooth round foot; red drinking-glass with attached
rings and white serpentine handles and short stem
Venetian art (late 18th-early 19th cent.)

Turin, Museo Civico

INDEXES

INDEX OF OBJECTS, PLACES, PERSONS
AND SUBJECTS

LIST OF ILLUSTRATIONS

241

COLOUR ILLUSTRATIONS

Frontispiece: Venetian glass table-ware, in a 14th century mosaic, detail from 'Herod's Feast' (1342–1354). Venice, Basilica di San Marco (Baptistery).

Plate

1　Two-handled amphora of ovoid shape without foot; produced by pouring into a mould and subsequently polishing with the grindstone (from Felsinian tombs dating from the 6th century B.C.). Phoenician art (6th century B.C.). Bologna, Museo Civico.

2　Small jug of 'oinochoe' type and small amphora of vitreous paste, the former with round flat foot, the latter with a small discoid foot, with poured polychrome decoration (from an Etruscan tomb). Etruscan art (?) (5th century B.C.). Bologna, Museo Civico.

3　Small 'oinochoe' type amphora with handle of green glass applied to a body of coloured pastes; technique combining moulding and pouring. Egyptian or Mediterranean art (ca. 2nd century B.C.). Solid block of iridescent glass. Roman art (?) (1st century A.D.). Murano, Museo Vetrario.

4　Two small plates of 'millefiori' type and small footless bowl with painted decorations. Alexandrian art (1st century A.D.). Turin, Museo Greco-Romano.

5　Cinerary urn with flat lid, of green glass. Roman art (1st–2nd century A.D.) Murano, Museo Vetrario.

6　Small balm flask in the shape of a bird, and spherical cinerary urn with bell-shaped lid. Roman art (1st–2nd century A.D.). Bologna, Museo Civico.

7　Beaker in the shape of a truncated cone with an embossed pattern blown in a metal mould. Flask and bottle of translucent glass. Roman art (1st–2nd century A.D.). Bologna, Museo Civico.

8　Small vase and bulbous bottle with conical neck; translucent iridescent glass. Roman art (1st–2nd century A.D.). Murano, Museo Vetrario.

9　Small footed bowl with two handles and bulbous bottle with long neck decorated with applied horizontal threads. Roman art (1st–2nd century A.D.). Murano, Museo Vetrario.

10　Bottle with long neck and bottle of square section, of blown glass. Small two-handled bowl with low foot, pressed and finished with the grindstone, after the 'pterotoi' type. Roman art (1st–2nd century A.D.). Bologna, Museo Civico.

11　Blown glass bottle with handle, speckled with white. Small gadrooned bowl blown on mould. Roman art (1st–2nd century A.D.). Bologna, Museo Civico.

12　Bottles of various shapes and sizes of transparent blown glass. Roman art (1st–2nd century A.D.). Murano, Museo Vetrario.

13　Footless cup with handle of greenish-blue glass. Roman art (1st–2nd century A.D.). Murano, Museo Vetrario.

14　Bottle of square section of transparent glass. Small bottle of opaque glass with handle. Roman art (1st–2nd century A.D.). Small bottle with square base, and beating a seal (the figure of Mercury). Turin, Museo Greco-Romano.

15　Bulbous cinerary urn of coloured glass. Roman art (1st–2nd century A.D.). Bologna, Museo Civico.

16　Spherical urn with conical lid and rounded foot, moulded and finished with the grindstone. Small footless bowl worked in the same way. Roman art (1st–2nd century A.D.). Turin, Museo Greco-Romano.

17　Double balm flask with threads applied in a continuous spiral. Syrian art (4th century A.D.). Small animal in blown glass and small vase with footless spherical body and handle. Roman art (3rd–4th century A.D.). Murano, Museo Vetrario.

18　Fragment of a plaque engraved with a battle scene; thick glass cut with the wheel. Hellenistic art (3rd century A.D.). Murano, Museo Vetrario.

19　Fragment of a bowl of translucent glass, bearing a hunting scene engraved with the grindstone. Alexandrian art (ca. 3rd–4th century A.D.). Murano, Museo Vetrario.

20　Jug of thick glass; exhumed in Murano (1878), perhaps a rare specimen of local production (ca. 14th century). Murano, Museo Vetrario.

21　Nuptial goblet attributed to the Baroviers, decorated with portraits of the bride and bridegroom and allegorical scenes in multicoloured and gold enamels: we see here the 'Fountain of Love'. Venetian art (ca. 1460–70). Murano, Museo Vetrario.

22　Liturgical chalice with a high foot, the lower part of the bowl decorated with prominent ribs in imitation of metal types; enamel decoration representing the 'Flight into Egypt', the 'Adoration of the Magi' and two medallions with busts of prophets. Venetian art (ca. 1460). Bologna, Museo Civico.

23　Nuptial goblet painted in enamel with medallions of the bride and bridegroom inside laurel wreaths, and cupids. Venetian art (ca. 1480). London, British Museum.

24　Goblet with a high foot and cylindrical body; enamel decoration depicting the 'Triumph of Justice'. Venetian art (ca. 1480). Florence, Museo Nazionale.

25　Nuptial goblet with a low foot, painted with polychrome and gold enamels depicting the 'Procession of Venus' (?) in a landscape. Venetian art (ca. 1480). London, British Museum.

26　Hanging mosque lamp in the shape of a bell; enamel decorations showing geometrical motifs and Arabic inscriptions. Syrian art (15th century). Florence, Museo Nazionale.

27　Jug and small pail of transparent glass decorated in polychrome enamels with plant patterns. Venetian art (late 15th century). Murano, Museo Vetrario.

28　Ribbed chalice with high base in the shape of a bell; small enamel decorations. Venetian art (late 15th century). Bologna, Museo Civico.

29　Beaker with moulded ribs decorated with enamel dots and scales round the rim; traces of gilding. Venetian art (late 15th century). Turin, Museo Civico.

PHOTOGRAPHIC CREDITS

GENERAL INDEX

THE FIRST ITALIAN EDITION OF THIS VOLUME
WAS PUBLISHED UNDER THE AUSPICES OF THE
BANCA NAZIONALE DEL LAVORO

Printed July 15, 1961, in Milan

COLLABORATORS

CARTIERA VENTURA, CARTIERA BURGO, ZINCOGRAFIA
ALTIMANI, S.A.E.S., STABILIMENTO GRAFICO MARIETTI,
ARTI GRAFICHE MILANESI, LEGATORIA TORRIANI

THE COLOUR REPRODUCTIONS WERE MADE EXPRESSLY
FOR ELECTA EDITRICE BY 'ARTE E COLORE' AND
FINE ART ENGRAVERS